PRACTICE TESTS FOR PROFICIENCY

FIRST SERIES

Margaret Archer
Enid Nolan-Woods

Nelson

Thomas Nelson and Sons Ltd.
Lincoln Way Windmill Road
Sunbury-on-Thames Middlesex TW16 7HP

P O Box 73146 Nairobi Kenya

P O Box 943, Kingston, Jamaica

Thomas Nelson (Australia) Ltd.
19–39 Jeffcott Street West Melbourne
Victoria 3003

Thomas Nelson and Sons (Canada) Ltd.
81 Curlew Drive Don Mills Ontario

Thomas Nelson (Nigeria) Ltd.
8 Ilupeju Bypass PMB 1303 Ikeja Lagos

© 1976 Margaret Archer and Enid Nolan-Woods
First published 1976
Reprinted 1977, 1978 (twice), 1979 (twice)
Students' Book 0 17 555153 7
Teacher's Book 0 17 555154 5

All Rights Reserved. No part of this publication may be reproduced, stored in a retrieval system, or transmitted, in any form or by any means, electronic, mechanical, photocopying, recording or otherwise, without the prior permission of Thomas Nelson and Sons Limited.

Phototypeset by Filmtype Services Limited, Scarborough, Yorkshire

ACKNOWLEDGEMENTS

We are grateful to the following for permission to reproduce copyright material:
The Hamlyn Publishing Group Ltd., for a passage from *Painting as a Pastime* by Sir Winston Churchill; The Estate of H. G. Wells for a passage from *The Country of the Blind* by H. G. Wells; The Oxford University Press for a passage from *Lark Rise to Candleford* by Flora Thompson; Mrs George Bambridge and The Macmillan Company of London and Basingstoke for a passage from *Drums of the Fore and Aft* by Rudyard Kipling; Granada Publishing Ltd. for a passage from *Elephant Bill* by J. H. Williams, published by Rupert Hart-Davis Ltd.; George Allen & Unwin Ltd., for a passage from *Human Robots in Myth and Science* by John Cotten; Sir Rupert Hart-Davis for a passage from *Portrait of a Man with Red Hair* by Hugh Walpole; and Miss D. E. Collins for a passage from "The Doom of the Darnaways" (in *The Incredulity of Father Brown*) by G. K. Chesterton.

All photographs are by D. J. Lewcock

Recorded material for this book is available from the publishers.

Also by Margaret Archer and Enid Nolan-Woods
Practice Tests for First Certificate English Books 1–3.
Cambridge Certificate English—a course for First Certificate.
Practice Tests for Proficiency Second Series.

Printed in Great Britain by A. Wheaton & Co. Ltd, Exeter

CONTENTS

FOREWORD

The object of this book is to provide students preparing for the Cambridge Certificate of Proficiency in English with complete practice in the Written and Oral papers. Each of the five tests consists of three Written and two Oral papers as follows:

WRITTEN PAPERS

Paper 1 **Composition** (3 hours)

> **Section A** A selection of Composition subjects is given based on description, narrative, argument and discussion. Students are normally required to write two compositions, one of each type, in the examination.
>
> **Section B** A passage on which the questions asked are designed to test the student's understanding and perception of different styles of writing.

Paper 2 Reading Comprehension ($1\frac{1}{4}$ hours)

> **Section A** Forty multiple choice questions testing vocabulary and usage.
>
> **Section B** Twenty multiple choice questions based on two texts. These can be used as testing material or as a means of expanding the student's vocabulary and general comprehension.

Paper 3 Use of English (3 hours)

> **Section A** This consists of a number of Units offering practice in a variety of English structures and usage.
>
> **Section B** One or more prose passages selected to test the student's ability to understand, interpret and summarise.
>
> **Section C** A composition to be written in a style appropriate to a given form i.e. a report, newspaper article, reply to letter, advertisement etc.

ORAL PAPERS

Paper 4 Listening Comprehension (45 minutes approx.)

> Four unseen passages with five multiple choice questions on each passage. The student should be given time to study the relevant questions before each reading. Each passage is read to the student twice at normal speed, allowing time between and after the readings to answer and check the questions.

Paper 5 Interview (12 minutes)

> **Section A** (5 mins. approx.) The student is asked to look at a photograph. He will then be expected to answer questions about it and discuss points arising from them.

Section B (2 mins. approx.) The student will be asked to speak on one of three topics presented to him before the Interview. He will be allowed about 15 minutes to prepare this beforehand. He may make a few written notes, but must not write a prepared speech.

Section C (2–3 mins. approx.) The student reads one part of a dialogue, the other part being read by the teacher. The student should be given time to prepare his part before reading. Particular attention should be paid to intonation, stress and rhythm.

Section D (2–3 mins. approx.) In this part of the examination the student will be expected to make a suitable response to *three* different situations. In these Tests *five* situations have been given to enable the teacher to cover a wider variety of situations when preparing students for the examination.

TEST ONE

Answer questions 1, 2 and 3. You should spend about the same amount of time on each.

Section A

1. **Either** (*a*) Write an account of any experience that has been decisive in influencing your way of life.

   or (*b*) Loneliness – its problems and how to combat them.

2. **Either** (*a*) Discuss the problem of living in high rise flats in cities and how this might be solved.

   or (*b*) Sex and Violence: Comment on the influence such films may or may not have on present day society.

Section B

3. Read the following passage, and then answer the questions which follow it:

It would be interesting if some real authority investigated carefully the part which memory plays in painting. We look at the object with an intent regard, then at the palette, and thirdly at the canvas. The canvas receives a message dispatched usually a few seconds before from the natural object. But it has come
5 through a post office en route. It has been transmitted in code. It has been turned from light into paint. It reaches the canvas a cryptogram. Not until it has been placed in its correct relation to everything else that is on the canvas can it be deciphered, is its meaning apparent, is it translated once again from mere pigment into light. And the light this time is not of Nature but of Art. The whole
10 of this considerable process is carried through on the wings or the wheels of memory. In most cases we think it is the wings – airy and quick like a butterfly from flower to flower. But all heavy traffic and all that has to go a long journey must travel on wheels.
In painting in the open air the sequence of actions is so rapid that the
15 process of translation into and out of pigment may seem to be unconscious. But all the greatest landscapes have been painted indoors, and often long after the first impressions were gathered. In a dim cellar the Dutch or Italian master recreated the gleaming ice of a Netherlands carnival or the lustrous sunshine of Venice or the Campagna. Here, then, is required a formidable memory of the
20 visual kind. Not only do we develop our powers of observation, but also those of carrying the record – of carrying it through an extraneous medium and of reproducing it, hours, days, or even months after the scene has vanished or the sunlight died.

I was told by a friend that when Whistler guided a school in Paris he made
25 his pupils observe their model on the ground floor, and then run upstairs and
paint their picture piece by piece on the floor above. As they became more
proficient, he put their easels up a storey higher, till at last the *élite* were scampering with their decision up six flights into the attic – praying it would not evaporate
on the way. This is, perhaps, only a tale. But it shows effectively of what
30 enormous importance a trained, accurate, retentive memory must be to an
artist; and conversely what a useful exercise painting may be for the development
of an accurate and retentive memory.

There is no better exercise for the would-be artist than to study and devour
a picture, and then, without looking at it again, to attempt the next day to
35 reproduce it. Nothing can more exactly measure the progress both of observation and of memory. It is still harder to compose out of many separate, well-
retained impressions, aided though they be by sketches and colour notes, a new,
complete conception. But this is the only way in which great landscapes have
been painted – or can be painted.

(*a*) "It reaches the canvas a cryptogram." (l. 6)
Why is the writer's use of the word "cryptogram" particularly apt in this
context?

(*b*) "And the light this time is not of Nature but of Art." What does the author
mean by saying this?

(*c*) What distinction does the writer make between "the wings" and "the
wheels" of memory?

(*d*) Comment on the writer's statement that "all the greatest landscapes have
been painted indoors".

(*e*) In the sentence ". . . till at last the *élite* were scampering with their decision
up six flights of stairs . . ." why is the word *scampering* used by the writer?

(*f*) Explain the difference between the two statements:

(a) "But it shows effectively of what enormous importance a trained,
accurate, retentive memory must be to an artist."

(b) ". . . what a useful exercise painting may be for the development of an
accurate or retentive memory."

(*g*) "Nothing can more exactly measure the progress both of observation and
memory."
What is the connection of this statement with the writer's general theme?

PAPER 2: READING COMPREHENSION (1¼ hours)

Section A

In this section you must choose the word or phrase, A, B, C, D or E which best completes each sentence. **Give one answer only** to each question.

1   John says that his present job does not provide him with enough _____ for his organising ability.
   A   scope   B   space   C   capacity   D   range   E   extension

2   Accuracy is _____ to the programming of computers.
   A   elemental   B   elementary   C   fundamental
   D   characteristic   E   influential

3   The Government's motion on Pension Increases _____ by a large majority.
   A   was dismissed   B   was defeated   C   was discarded
   D   was deposed   E   was dispersed

4   The vacuum cleaner is a valuable labour-saving _____ for the busy housewife.
   A   piece   B   motor   C   engine   D   device   E   instrument

5   I have no hesitation in saying that Miss Jones is a most responsible and _____ worker.
   A   conscientious   B   consequential   C   conscious
   D   conclusive   E   considerable

6   If you don't lift that saucepan carefully, it will spill and you may _____ yourself.
   A   skim   B   peel   C   scald   D   skin   E   singe

7   The generation _____ makes it difficult for parents to understand their children's opinions.
   A   division   B   gap   C   partition   D   interval   E   separation

8   The completion of the new Town Hall has been _____ owing to a strike.
   A   held off   B   held down   C   held in   D   held up
   E   held on

9   Colour-blind people often find it difficult _____ between blue and green.
   A   to separate   B   to compare   C   to contrast   D   to relate
   E   to distinguish

10   Most great artists are exceptionally _____ people.
   A   sensitized   B   sensitive   C   sensuous   D   sensory
   E   senseless

11   Mr Sanders has been asked _____ the next meeting of the Library Committee.
   A   to present   B   to preside   C   to chair   D   to deal
   E   to lead

12   It has always been the _____ of our firm to encourage staff to take part in social activities.
   A   policy   B   plan   C   campaign   D   procedure   E   plot

13 The statue in the city square _____ the soldiers who lost their lives in the Great War.
A celebrates   B commemorates   C reminds   D recaptures
E remembers

14 On religious feast days _____ of the local saint is carried in procession through the streets of the town.
A a copy   B a prototype   C a design   D an effigy
E a reproduction

15 It is a pity that George is so _____ in his choice of friends.
A indifferent   B undefined   C undistinguished
D indiscriminate   E indistinguishable

16 Inflation is the first problem that the new Government will have _____.
A to grip   B to tackle   C to seize   D to grasp
E to clasp

17 Simon has never had a settled career, he has always lived _____.
A at the ready   B on the turn   C round the bend
D by his wits   E up his sleeve

18 The diamond in my grandmother's ring was quite _____. It was a perfect specimen.
A spotless   B refined   C unstained   D flawless
E untarnished

19 When his father died, John _____ a great deal of money.
A went into   B looked into   C made into   D brought into
E came into

20 Our Borough Council has increased our _____ by 45% this year.
A levies   B dues   C rates   D capitations   E accounts

21 Reminders must be sent out to all customers whose accounts are more than a month _____.
A indebted   B overdue   C unpaid   D unbalanced
E insolvent

22 The burglar was taken to the Police Station and _____ with breaking and entering.
A indicted   B prosecuted   C accused   D tried
E charged

23 The sea was so _____ that some of the passengers in the pleasure boat felt seasick.
A gusty   B breezy   C runny   D wavy   E choppy

24 It has been decided to hold a Public _____ into the cause of the accident.
A Inquiry   B Autopsy   C Interrogation   D Trial
E Examination

25 Peter is always _____ about how well he plays football.
A vaunting   B puffing   C flaunting   D parading
E boasting

26 The deer in the Park are so accustomed to being fed by visitors that they are quite _____.
A trained   B tame   C servile   D nerveless   E domestic

27   The lecturer spoke so fast that I found it hard _____ what he was saying.
A   to take in   B   to take out   C   to take over   D   to take up
E   to take away

28   Visitors to the Zoo are asked not _____ the monkeys.
A   to fret   B   to nag   C   to tease   D   to bite   E   to peck

29   Owing to the warm weather, there has been _____ of strawberries this year.
A   a swarm   B   an overflow   C   a redundancy   D   an affluence
E   a glut

30   I like classical music, but I don't _____ to know anything about it.
A   assume   B   pretend   C   imagine   D   simulate   E   believe

31   Georgina will never become a good actress until she stops taking _____ to any form of criticism.
A   reproach   B   exemption   C   exception   D   resentment
E   indignation

32   We are forwarding the goods in _____ with your instructions.
A   agreement   B   accordance   C   accord   D   concord
E   assent

33   In response to our advertisement, two couples are coming _____ the flat tomorrow afternoon.
A   to turn over   B   to get over   C   to run over   D   to see over
E   to pass over

34   The ambulance men took the injured climber down the mountain on _____.
A   a stretcher   B   a cot   C   a couch   D   a hammock
E   a bedstead

35   Many essential foods had _____ during World War II.
A   to be divided   B   to be allotted   C   to be rationed
D   to be proportioned   E   to be separated

36   Mr Stevens assured me that he never bought _____ that were advertised on TV.
A   productions   B   products   C   projects   D   prospects
E   projections

37   While he was in hospital, the soldier's wound _____ twice a day.
A   was healed   B   was changed   C   was dressed   D   was cured
E   was relieved

38   The President's personal _____ never left his side during the State Visit.
A   sentinel   B   protector   C   defender   D   bodyguard
E   lifeguard

39   The condition of the castle walls _____ over the years.
A   has deteriorated   B   has depreciated   C   has decomposed
D   has degenerated   E   has declined

40   Manufacturers hope that the Motor Show will _____ car sales in Britain.
A   lift   B   inflate   C   boom   D   advance   E   boost

Section B

After each of the passages in this section there are a number of questions or unfinished statements about the passage, each with four suggested answers. Choose the one you think best. **Give one answer only** to each question. Read each passage right through before choosing your answers.

First Passage

The train began to slow down among the fields. I looked out and saw a wooden platform, and a board with "Aberdovey" on it. And there, too, was Arthur looking anxiously up and down the train. With him was a large vicar, overflowing with boisterous greetings, as I got out.

5   "We may as well walk up," said Arthur, "I fear there's no taxi to be had." As we left the station he pointed to a black box on wheels, drawn by an unbelievably old horse, driven by an unbelievably old man. "That is the Aberdovey bus plying between station and town. You tell old Rushell where you want to be put down, climb in, bang the door as a sign that you are safe, and in time
10 he starts. We shall see him presently on the road; it's about all the traffic we have."

It was a goodish walk from the station, for the town straggled along between the hills and the estuary, including on its way a real port with a bright-funnelled little steamer tied up at the quay. I was amused with the walk and glad to stretch
15 my legs after being cooped up so long. The vicar accompanied us most of the way, not from parochial duty, as I at first imagined, but, as I learned later, because he had nothing else to do, and my arrival was a bit of an event, a trifle to add to the gossip. I was amazed at the way in which both he and Arthur turned on Welsh, as though from a tap, whenever they met an acquaintance, which
20 was about every hundred yards.

At last the vicar said good-bye. He was very stout and didn't want to do our final climb. The tiny house that Arthur had obtained for his mother was at the end of a tiny row, lodged precariously on a tiny ledge of the hillside. We could reach the house only by a rough and very steep path. At the open door stood
25 Mrs Hughes, with a "Well, well, well, and here you are at last!" It is curious how a mere tone of voice can make you feel at home at once. A meal was all ready, and as I fell upon it heartily I was able to amuse Arthur and his mother with the story of my journey; he, poor fellow, had been at the station since two o'clock, off and on.

41   The vicar who met Arthur at the station

    A   was bursting with news
    B   was overwhelmed with emotion
    C   welcomed him exuberantly
    D   greeted him unenthusiastically

42   The writer and his friends didn't think it was worth taking the bus because

    A   it didn't go far enough
    B   it only went from the station
    C   they didn't want to ride in a black box
    D   the horse was too old to walk uphill

43　According to Arthur, if you wanted to take the Aberdovey bus you had to

　　A　be content to go when the driver was ready
　　B　be ready to start on time
　　C　get in and give directions to the driver
　　D　signal to the driver when to get in

44　In line 12 of the passage the expression "a goodish walk" refers to

　　A　the pleasant scenery
　　B　the distance covered
　　C　the winding roads
　　D　the healthy air

45　From the passage we understand that the writer was glad to walk as

　　A　he liked walking long distances
　　B　he found walking amusing
　　C　he had long legs
　　D　he was stiff after his long journey

46　The writer first thought that the vicar accompanied Arthur and him

　　A　from boredom
　　B　from politeness
　　C　out of a sense of duty
　　D　to obtain information

47　The house that Arthur's mother lived in was

　　A　on a by-pass
　　B　on the highway
　　C　in a lay-by
　　D　off the beaten track

48　From information given in the passage, it would appear that

　　A　Arthur and the vicar spoke only Welsh
　　B　Only Arthur and the vicar spoke Welsh
　　C　Arthur and the vicar only spoke Welsh sometimes
　　D　Arthur and the vicar only spoke Welsh to each other

49　How do we know that Mrs Hughes was glad to meet the writer?

　　A　from the words she said
　　B　by the way she spoke
　　C　from her homely appearance
　　D　from her curious voice

50　What makes us think that the writer arrived later than expected?

　　A　she said the train had been delayed
　　B　Arthur had been waiting at the station since two o'clock
　　C　Arthur had had to make frequent trips to the station
　　D　she said the journey had been amusing

Second Passage

I assume that the desirability of a school book stall needs no urging. Many schools sell food and toys. If we do not sell books it is surely strange? Many schools serve areas where book shops do not exist and the only books brought before children for buying are the dubious selections of supermarkets. More-
5 over even in communities where a good book shop is available the guidance which can be given at the book stall is valuable, as we soon found.

Essentially the school book stall is an extension of the encouragement and guidance in private reading which is part of the work of the English teacher. The first essential then, in setting up shop is a teacher particularly interested in
10 children reading and in building up as wide as possible a knowledge of books to suit the school's range of pupils.   ·

Given the teacher, the next requirement is a bookseller willing to supply you. In some cases you will be able to obtain your books on credit, paying as you sell, but if the school can find a sum to purchase its stock, or at least a part of
15 it, this is a great help.

Having found your supplier you then approach the Publisher's Association for a Book Agent's licence. The licence entitles you to a discount on your purchases through your chosen supplier, the usual discount being 10 per cent with service. Service usually consists of delivery and a sale or return arrange-
20 ment, the latter essential in allowing you to be enterprising and experimental in your stock. Without service a slightly higher discount is given but the former arrangement is clearly preferable.

The biggest, indeed the only considerable, cost in running the book stall is the occasional theft of a book and this may well vary from school to school but the
25 presence of the teacher and the alertness of the assistants is largely deterrent, and the discount should cover this and any other smaller expenses. Browsing is essential. The books must be handled. You cannot keep them safe and immaculate behind glass.

For equipment the only essentials are some tables on which to display the
30 books and a cupboard to store them in. Incidentally an arrangement of books with covers rather than spines visible seems to be vastly more attractive and accessible to children who have not the habit of browsing. A single way out past the cash desk is helpful to security and we record details of each purchase in-cluding the age of the buyer both for reordering and as interesting information
35 on reading habits.

Initially we stocked two hundred titles and the selection has grown to close on a thousand. It is convenient if cash or credit allow you to have duplicate copies of popular titles. What is stocked must depend on the teacher in charge. What you are prepared to sell in the cause of encouraging interest in reading
40 will obviously be an individual judgment. Sales for their own sake are in the school context obviously purposeless and the teacher needs to be able to explain to interested parents why he thought a given book valuable for a certain child.

There are always more offers of help from pupils than we can accept. The assistants serve, recommend, order, make posters and arrange displays. Some
45 of the least able pupils have worked devotedly at the book stall.

Publicity is vital. We have two display cases on the school approach contain-ing forty books changed fortnightly and they arouse a lot of interest. Teachers' recommendations, book lists, beginnings of stories read to classes, do much. Some classes buy a book a week between them. The book stall is always open
50 on such occasions as Parents' Evenings.

We open twice a week in the lunch hour and we sell twenty to forty books a week, commercially not much but in our opinion well worth the effort.

51   The writer implies that the reason why a school needs a book stall is

    A   because children always choose the wrong books
    B   children find it difficult to choose books in a supermarket
    C   because children only like strange books
    D   children find it difficult to choose the right books

52   According to the passage the teacher who runs a book stall should be

    A   interested in reading children's books
    B   interested in children's ability to read
    C   interested in reading to children
    D   interested in writing children's books

53   The writer suggests that it is advantageous for the school to

    A   invest in a reasonable stock at the outset
    B   invest in surplus stock from a bookseller
    C   be able to sell books on credit
    D   be able to pay cash on delivery

54   Having obtained a licence the buyer is then entitled to

    A   select the bookseller of his choice
    B   retail books at a lower price
    C   be a member of the Publisher's Association
    D   buy books below the retail price

55   To what does "this may well vary" refer (1. 24)?

    A   The expenditure on books
    B   The number of books stolen
    C   The vigilance of the assistants
    D   The number of books stocked

56   In the opinion of the writer children should

    A   only touch books with clean hands
    B   spend their spare time looking at books
    C   look at books at their leisure
    D   only touch clean books

57   What is one of the ways of discovering the books that children prefer?

    A   by observing the children as they leave
    B   by recording the children's ages
    C   by noting which children buy books
    D   by noting which books children buy

58   "What is stocked must depend on" (1. 38)

    A   good taste
    B   considered opinion
    C   unanimous decision
    D   indiscriminate judgment

59 The writer considered one of the contributing factors to the successful running of the book stall was assistance from

    A over eager children
    B disabled children
    C children of low potential
    D children of all round ability

60 The school makes it possible for the children to know what books are available by

    A rearranging all of the books every two weeks
    B arranging fortnightly visits to the book stall
    C exhibiting books to advantage
    D holding regular exhibitions of books

PAPER 3: USE OF ENGLISH (3 hours)

SECTION A

1. Fill each of the numbered blanks in the passage with **one** suitable word.

At the end of the slope he _____ (1) a thousand feet and came down in the _____ (2) of snow upon a slope even steeper than the one _____ (3). Down this he was whirled, stunned and insensible, but without a _____ (4) broken in his body; and _____ (5) at last came to gentler slopes, and rolled out and lay _____ (6), buried in a softening heap of the white masses that had accompanied and saved him. He came _____ (7) with a dim fancy that he was ill in bed; then _____ (8) his position with a mountaineer's intelligence, and worked himself loose and, after a moment or _____ (9), he saw the stars. He rested flat on his chest for a space, _____ (10) where he was and _____ (11) had happened to him. He explored his limbs and discovered that several of his buttons were gone. His knife had gone from his pocket and his hat was lost _____ (12) he had tied it under his _____ (13). He decided that he _____ (14) had fallen, and looked

_____(15) to see, exaggerated by the ghastly light of the moon, the tremendous flight he had taken. For a while he _____(16) gazing blankly at that vast pale cliff _____(17) above. Its phantasmal, mysterious beauty held _____(18) for a space, and then he was _____(19) with a paroxysm of sobbing laughter. After a long interval, he became _____(20) that he was near the lower edge of the snow.

2. Finish each of the following sentences in such a way that it means exactly the same as the sentence printed before it.

Example: They say Mr Jones is a very good administrator

Answer: Mr Jones *is said to be a very good administrator*

Is it absolutely necessary to answer those letters today?

1 Do those letters ....?

It is impossible for me to catch an earlier train.

2 There is ....

How high do you think the tallest building in New York is?

3 What ....?

The Managing Director said very little about the proposed merger.

4 The proposed merger ....

I shan't accept that appointment if the salary is too low.

5 I shall only ....

Who is the owner of this briefcase?

6 Who does ....?

Increasing the tax on household goods is bound to cause trouble.

7 It's asking...

The doctor told Mary to tell her mother he would call in half an hour.

8 "Tell ....

Did anyone reply to your advertisement in the local paper last week?

9 Have there ....?

Music has never been one of John's interests.

10 John has ....

3. Fill each of the numbered blanks with a suitable word or phrase.

Example:
   Susan: I'm afraid John has failed his exam again.
   Philip: Well, it's his own fault, he *ought to have worked harder.*

1 "I think Julia ought to see a doctor, she ....
   very well lately."

2 "The more Mary has, ..."

3 "I couldn't get any answer when I rang Mr White. I think ....
   ...."

4 "Don't tell Gordon what Mary said about him, he ....
   ...."

5 After that argument with the Manager, it wouldn't have been surprising
   if Peterson ....

6 "When I'm trying to explain something to my students, nothing annoys
   me more ...."

7 I was walking along the street when I ....
   to a friend.

8 My father says that if he .... to go to University
   when he was young, he would be Prime Minister today.

9 Mark says he is going to buy a motor bicycle whether his father ....

....

10 Stephen will never be a good footballer, however much ....

....

4. For each of the sentences below, write a new sentence **as similar as possible in meaning to the original sentence,** but using the word given in capital letters.

Example: Nobody let me see her after the accident.
   ALLOWED

Answer: *I wasn't allowed to see her after the accident.*

1 Do you really have to catch the 9.30 train?
   NECESSARY

....

2 Miss Jones received £1000 for the injuries she sustained in the car accident.
   WAS

....

3 We didn't speak the language so we had to make signs.
   UNABLE

....

4 I'm certain it wasn't John you saw at the station.
   CAN'T

....

5 More reading would have improved his spelling.
   IF

....

6 Ask Professor Smith, I'm sure he'll know the answer.
   BOUND

....

7 Was the question of traffic control raised at the Council meeting?
   DID

....

8 Is it advisable to thaw frozen chicken before cooking it?
SHOULD

....

9 I wonder what's happened to John, he's never late as a rule.
THINK

....

10 In my opinion John and Mary paid far too much for that antique mirror.
WORTH

....

SECTION B

5. Read the following passage, and then answer the questions which follow it.

The study of the history of the forerunners of the modern Christmas card proves that the tradition of exchanging charms or small tokens of good luck at this time of the year goes back to very ancient times. In fact, we should have to go back to pre-Christian times, when the festival was not yet celebrated as the
5 anniversary of the Birth of Christ, but as a feast for the winter solstice. People then celebrated the reawakening of Nature, anticipating the coming of Spring and longer hours of daylight. They associated with it their various forms of belief in the victory of life over death, light over darkness and vegetation over snow and ice. The solstice season was the time of magic for men, and they could
10 then, from the signs of their gods, read portents and foretell coming events during the New Year. The feasts and rites aimed to propitiate the friendly and disarm the unfriendly gods or spirits. Actors and their plays, mistletoe and the kiss beneath it, the yule log and its lighting, a number of traditional dishes, such as the boar's head and mince pie, all have their origin in these ancient rites. It
15 is the nature of human customs and habits to survive long after their original meaning and significance have been forgotten.

Available archaeological material indicates that it was usual amongst the Egyptians to give small symbolic presents conveying wishes of good luck with allusions to the New Year. Small blue-glazed bottles were found in the tombs
20 of the Pharaohs, probably scent-flasks, bearing inscriptions about flowers and the approaching New Year.

In Rome it was an ancient custom for all those who were connected with a household to visit it on the first day of January to exchange greetings and presents. Originally these were branches of laurel or olive, picked from the
25 sacred groves. Later the presents usually took a more practical form, such as dates, figs and other edibles, which were sometimes coated with gold leaf and were symbolic of good luck for the New Year. Honey as a present meant the wish that the coming year should be as sweet to the recipient as honey itself. Later, however, a present of cash was considered even sweeter than honey,
30 pointing to the changing habits under the Caesars. The presents conveying the greetings were more and more frequently actual coins with a Janus head on them. (January was named after Janus, the two-headed God of the New Year.) These

coins with the Janus head were originally a valid currency and became perhaps the most popular tokens to express the compliments of the season.

35 The advent and spread of Christianity and the continued adherence to pagan January celebrations concurred for some time within the realm of Rome, but as time passed the pagan saturnalia was replaced by Christmas, the celebration of the birth of Christ. The Christian Christmas spirit introduced a slow but truly remarkable transformation, and seasonal elements which survived from
40 previous times were enriched by new meaning and content. This enabled them long to outlast the ancient gods, in whose cults they originated.

Besides the performed and vocal customs, the giving and receiving of tokens of good wishes continued, and remain a feature of the winter solstice. Generally speaking, those countries whose language belongs to the Latin group continued
45 to observe January 1st rather than Christmas Day as the appropriate date for the exchange of presents. In some European countries only New Year cards and visits sustained the Roman tradition. The New Year cards did not include references to Christmas and were sent out after the 25th, intended to arrive on New Year's Day.

50 The English seasonal greeting card was, on the other hand, different, since it conveniently combined Christmas and the New Year, with the emphasis on Christmas. These cards were meant to be delivered on or before Christmas Day and to convey greetings for the Christmas festivities and the following year, so unwittingly and from the very beginning emphasising the significance of the
55 Christmas festivities as in some way the successors of the old winter solstice celebrations.

1 When did the custom of celebrating the end of the year originate, and what was its purpose.

....

....

2 What effects were the winter feasts thought to have?

....

....

3 How do we know that the ancient Egyptians celebrated the New Year?

....

....

4 Why were coins with a Janus head on them considered appropriate as presents?

....

5 How did the winter celebrations change under Christianity?

....

6   What does "it" in line 7 refer to? ....

7   Who were able to "read portents" in line 10? ....

8   What does the word "it" refer to in line 14? ....

9   The word "those" in line 22 refers to ....

10 What were "the changing habits"? (l. 30) ....
    ....

11 What "concurred" in line 36? ....

12 The word "This" in line 40 refers to ....

13 Give an alternative phrase for "remain a feature" (l. 43) ....
    ....

14 Why do the New Year cards referred to in line 47 "not include references
    to Christmas"? ....

15 Why are presents not generally given on Christmas Day in some Latin
    speaking countries? ....
    ....

16 How was the English greeting card "different"? (l. 50) ....
    ....

17 What is implied by the word "unwittingly" in line 54? ....
    ....

18 In a paragraph of not more than 100 words describe how modern English
    Christmas cards are "the successors of the old winter solstice celebrations".
    (ll. 55–56)..
    ....
    ....
    ....
    ....
    ....
    ....

....

....

....

SECTION C

6. The following report appeared in the Newchester *Daily Gazette*. Write a letter to the Rev. Eddison protesting at the annoyance being caused to local residents by the young people at the Reception Centre and make some constructive suggestions on how this should be dealt with. Your letter should be not more than 150 words.

In view of the increasing number of homeless youngsters roaming our city in search of work, the Newchester Borough Council have recently opened a Reception Centre at St Peter's Vicarage where those in need can receive help and guidance. Provision has been made for short-term stay and the Centre will be manned night and day to give assistance in finding work and suitable living accommodation. Readers of this newspaper who feel they would like to help in this venture are invited to write direct to the Rev. Eddison, St Peter's Vicarage, Easter Lane, Newchester.

PAPER 4: LISTENING COMPREHENSION (40 minutes)

The passages on which these questions are based will be found in the Appendix.

First Passage

1 From the text we understand that the two artists were looking at a

   A   painting that interested them
   B   view that interested them
   C   painting of a seascape
   D   view that one of them had painted

2 From the information given we receive the impression that one of the artists

   A   knew more about the landscape than the other
   B   knew more about local painters than the other
   C   was celebrated for his landscape paintings
   D   was celebrated for his paintings of London

3 The sombre colours in the scene appeared "more mysterious than gold" because they were

   A contrasted with the sand
   B blurred by the sunset
   C illumined by the sunset
   D reflected in the sand

4 What was a curious feature of the lower part of the building in the scene?

   A the large holes in the walls
   B the drawn blinds in the windows
   C the light in one of the windows
   D the absence of any light

5 From what Martin Wood said it appears that the building

   A had been inhabited by ghosts
   B ought to be inhabited by ghosts
   C was inhabited by people who liked ghosts
   D was inhabited by ghost-like people

Second Passage

6 What did Inspector Harrison do immediately after he heard the screams?

   A retraced his steps
   B turned aside
   C continued straight ahead
   D ran ahead of Briggs

7 How did Briggs guess that the screams had come from the direction of the pond? He heard

   A someone running into the water
   B someone screaming from the house
   C a sound that he identified
   D a sound that he didn't recognise

8 From the information given how do we know that the woman by the pond was in a distressed condition?

   A she was kneeling on the ground
   B she was making a low sound
   C she wasn't wearing any clothes
   D she was dragging a boy on to her lap

9 How was the boy in the passage prevented from dying?

   A his breathing was stimulated
   B he was given oxygen
   C his heart was examined
   D his pulse was taken

10. When they entered the house, the policemen found it difficult to see because
    A   it was too dim to distinguish anything clearly
    B   their eyes had to adjust to the light
    C   the hall was full of shadows
    D   the staircase blocked their view

Third Passage

11 Why does the writer describe the mist in the fields as a "transparent wall"?
    A   it reflected the light from the cottage windows
    B   it was reflected in the cottage windows
    C   it could be seen through
    D   it couldn't be walked through

12 How did Stephen feel about the damp weather that evening?
    A   he was afraid of the cold
    B   he found it depressing
    C   he welcomed it
    D   he regretted the recent fine spell

13 From the footprints Stephen deduced that whoever had cut the plants had
    A   cut them at random
    B   selected them carefully
    C   tried to uproot them
    D   trodden on all of them

14 It seems likely from the passage that
    A   only Francis could have picked the plants
    B   Francis had worn boots to pick the plants
    C   the plants could only have been picked by someone in boots
    D   someone in boots had managed to reach the plants

15 Why do you think people frequently used the path through the wood?
    A   it saved time getting to the village
    B   it cut through the village
    C   it was the safest way to the village
    D   it was cut off from the village

Fourth Passage

16   From the passage we understand that Carl Sagan writes

    A   forcefully and complexly
    B   elaborately and literally
    C   simply and humorously
    D   snobbishly and cleverly

17   Carl Sagan suggests that modern man

    A   is very confused about the origin of the Earth
    B   might possibly reach life outside the Earth
    C   believes it is possible to step off the Earth
    D   is historically incapable of exploring the universe

18   How much does Sagan think America should spend on Space Exploration?

    A   more than she does at present
    B   less than she does at present
    C   as much as England did in the sixteenth century
    D   all of her gross national income

19   It would appear that the public Sagan hopes to attract

    A   are interested in UFO spotting
    B   are only interested in science fiction
    C   are unable to write science fiction
    D   have a reasonable grounding in science

20   The text seems to imply that other forms of life in the cosmos

    A   have never existed
    B   have all died out
    C   may exist in the future
    D   are in existence

PAPER 5: INTERVIEW (12 minutes)

Section A *Photograph*

Look at this photograph carefully and be prepared to answer some questions about it.

Describe the scene in the picture.
What equipment, including clothes, would you need for a day's sailing?
Would you like to take the place of one of the men? Give your reasons.

Reasons for the popularity of sailing.
Increasing use of the sea for leisure activities.
Need for provision of more Marinas.
Competitive racing versus family pastime.

Section B *Topics*

Choose one of the following topics and prepare to give your views on it, for
1½ to 2 minutes. You may make notes, but do not try to write out a whole speech.

1   Discuss the advantages and disadvantages of air travel.

2   Should married women go out to work?

3   How are the public's buying habits influenced by advertising?

Section C *Dialogue*

(Prepare yourself to read the part of MIRANDA. The teacher will read the
other part.)

Nicholas: You never cease to amaze me, Miranda. Every time I see you,
            you're different.

MIRANDA: Isn't that what Napoleon said about Josephine: "Age cannot
            wither nor custom stale her infinite variety"?

Nicholas: Actually it was Antony and Cleopatra – the Shakespeare version.

MIRANDA: It doesn't matter who said it. The point is that no woman should
            ever allow herself to be typecast – devoted wife, dedicated subur-
            ban housewife, liberated career girl – it's inhibiting. People classify
            you as this or that, and they don't expect you to have any opinions,
            except what they've decided you ought to have.

Nicholas: I wasn't thinking so much of your opinions, as your appearance.
            When I make a date with you, I'm never quite sure what girl I'm
            taking out.

MIRANDA: That just shows how narrow-minded you are. You're expecting
            a delicate doe-eyed beauty and you're thrown because you're
            confronted with a blonde bombshell, or a female in twinset and
            pearls who looks like the honorary secretary of her local hockey
            club. It's the greatest mistake in the world for men to have pre-
            conceived ideas about women.

Nicholas: Nevertheless, you must admit it's a bit disconcerting, especially
            as I don't much care for women hockey players, or blonde bomb-
            shells either for that matter.

MIRANDA: That's because you're afraid of them – or, at least, afraid of what
            you think they represent. Any woman worth her salt knows that
            the best way to attract a man is to be a constant challenge to his
            masculinity.

Nicholas: What's your attitude then to Women's Lib.?

MIRANDA: Personally, I've always been totally liberated. It's utter nonsense
            all this talk about Women's Rights. Women are infinitely superior
            to men and they've always known it. The only wonder is that the
            pretence of male superiority has been kept up for so long.

Nicholas: You wouldn't agree then that we still live in a man's world?

MIRANDA: Of course not. It suits women to pander to men's idea of themselves as the stronger sex. The most effective weapon in the world is femininity and it would take a braver man than you to question that.

Section D *Situations*

1 You are involved in a slight accident in which your car is damaged. You think that the driver of the other car is responsible. Tell him why you think so. Be polite but firm.

2 Your boss is retiring and you have been asked to collect money for a presentation. What do you say to your colleagues in the office?

3 You are passing along a quiet street when you see smoke coming from a closed shop. Go to the nearest house and ask if you can telephone the Fire Brigade. Explain your reasons.

4 A man arrives to repair your television set. Explain what is wrong.

5 You are travelling by bus but when you get off at your destination, you realise you have left your suitcase on the bus. Go to the Lost Property Office, explain what has happened and describe the contents of the case.

TEST TWO

Answer questions 1, 2 and 3. You should spend about the same amount of time on each.

Section A

1. Either (*a*) Discuss the effect of the seasons on mankind.

or (*b*) Imagine how you would feel and behave if you were the last person alive on Earth.

2. Either (*a*) Discuss the role of the artist in society.

or (*b*) Are two parents necessary for a child to develop successfully?

Section B

3. Read the following passage, and then answer the questions which follow it:

There are certain philosophers who have fallen into the habit of speaking slightingly of Time and Space. Time, they say, is only a poor concept of ours corresponding to no ultimate reality, and Space is little better. They are merely mental receptacles into which we put our sensations. We are assured that could
5 we get at the right point of view we should see that real existence is timeless. Of course we cannot get at the right point of view, but that does not matter.

It is easy to understand how philosophers can talk in that way, for familiarity with great subjects breeds contempt; but we of the laity cannot dismiss either Time or Space so cavalierly. Having once acquired the time-habit, it is difficult
10 to see how we could live without it. We are accustomed to use the minutes and hours as stepping-stones, and we pick our way from one to another. If it were not for them, we should find ourselves at once beyond our depth. It is the succession of events that makes them interesting. There is a delightful transitoriness about everything, and yet the sense that there is more where it all comes from. To the
15 unsophisticated mind Eternity is not the negation of Time; it is having all the time one wants. And why may not the unsophisticated mind be as nearly right in such matters as any other?

In a timeless existence there would be no distinction between now and then, before and after. Yesterdays and todays would be merged in one featureless
20 Forever. When we met one another it would be impertinent to ask, "How do you do?" The chilling answer would be: "I do not do; I am." There would be nothing more to say to one who had reduced his being to such bare metaphysical first principles. I much prefer living in Time, where there are circumstances and incidents to give variety to existence. There is a dramatic instinct in all of us that

25 must be satisfied. We watch with keen interest for what is coming next. We would rather have long waits than have no shifting of the scenes, and all the actors on the stage at once, doing nothing.

(*a*) What in the opinion of certain philosophers is the function of Time and Space?

(*b*) "We are accustomed to use the minutes and hours as stepping stones." Comment on this statement (in line 11.)

(*c*) What is meant by the phrase: ". . . a delightful transitoriness about everything" (in lines 13–14)?

(*d*) Explain the distinction the writer makes in the following statement (in line 15.)
". . . Eternity is not the negation of Time; it is having all the time one wants."

(*e*) In what ways does the writer suggest that a timeless existence would differ from our own?

(*f*) Comment on the use of the word "chilling" (in line 21.)

(*g*) It would seem that the writer feels that living in Time enlivens our existence. Give reasons.

PAPER 2: READING COMPREHENSION (1¼ hours)

Section A

In this section you must choose the word or phrase, A, B, C, D or E which best completes each sentence. **Give one answer only** to each question.

1 Alan is _____ to think he is the only person who knows the best restaurants in London.
A prejudiced B apt C impressed D conducive
E subjected

2 The firm will go bankrupt if it cannot meet its _____.
A duties B penalties C liabilities D promises
E charges

3 Mr. Stone would be glad if you would call at any time _____ to yourself.
A appropriate B expedient C convenient D likely
E opportune

4 The intruder was badly _____ by the guard dog at the factory.
A mauled B damaged C eaten D torn E violated

5 The _____ in television sales is causing some concern to the manufacturers.
A deficit B slump C offset D deterioration E poverty

6 My father, who is not easily surprised, was quite _____ when he heard the result of the Election.
A given over B put round C brought about D turned up
E taken aback

7 The spy _____ the desk in an attempt to find the secret documents.
A looted   B ransacked   C invaded   D pilfered
E kidnapped

8 The Examination Board have recently changed the _____ for the Diploma in English Literature.
A programme   B plan   C brochure   D compendium
E syllabus

9 When my grandfather died, his house was put up to _____.
A market   B bargain   C auction   D offer   E disposal

10 Before the operation on her heart, Mrs. Jackson was asked to give the name and address of her _____.
A friends and relations   B next of kin   C kith and kin
D flesh and blood   E friends and neighbours

11 A scholarship has been endowed _____ the memory of Father Lawrence's work among the mentally retarded.
A to foster   B to prolong   C to persist   D to perpetuate
E to encourage

12 We shall have to tighten our _____ if we are to overcome the present economic crisis.
A belts   B waists   C straps   D braces   E laces

13 Mary looks the picture of _____ since she returned from her holiday.
A wholesomeness   B well-being   C healthiness   D health
E wealth

14 The instructions for making this jumper are so complicated that I can't make _____ of them.
A top to bottom   B head or tail   C half and half
D up and down   E plain and purl

15 If you never do any work, you will only have yourself _____ if you fail your examination.
A to fault   B to reprove   C to upbraid   D to mistake
E to blame

16 The detective remained _____ behind the door waiting for his assailant.
A static   B unmoved   C motionless   D immovable
E lifeless

17 The judge _____ the burglar to two years' imprisonment.
A charged   B convicted   C accused   D sentenced
E committed

18 My brother is an enthusiastic photographer, and _____ all his own film.
A develops   B takes   C perfects   D illustrates
E glosses

19 A Member of Parliament has to spend a great deal of time answering letters from his _____.
A candidates   B patrons   C constituents   D selectors
E representatives

20   At the conclusion of the Summit Meeting, a disarmament _____ was
signed by all the major Powers.
A   undertaking   B   proposal   C   proposition   D   treaty
E   prescription

21   If we don't have some rain soon, there will be a serious _____ in the west
of England.
A   flood   B   famine   C   drought   D   aridity   E   dehydration

22   I have just learnt that my neighbour is an authority on _____ architecture.
A   middle-aged   B   mediaeval   C   archaic   D   antiquarian
E   antediluvian

23   I am _____ whether to go to Italy for my holiday or not.
A   in two minds   B   on one hand   C   at cross purposes
D   at sixes and sevens   E   on all fours

24   My husband has just _____ to Sales Manager of his firm.
A   been upraised   B   been preferred   C   been elevated
D   been advanced   E   been promoted

25   There are some very beautiful _____ glass windows in Canterbury
Cathedral.
A   marked   B   stained   C   modelled   D   drawn   E   designed

26   During the recent strike the workers _____ the factory gates so that no one
could gain admission.
A   hindered   B   impeded   C   restrained   D   picketed
E   intercepted

27   My neighbour and his wife have decided _____ to Australia.
A   to migrate   B   to immigrate   C   to emigrate
D   to expatriate   E   to deport

28   When I was at school we had to learn a poem _____ every week.
A   by hand   B   by ear   C   by mouth   D   by heart   E   by eye

29   Jane is far too _____, she must learn to consider her actions beforehand.
A   impulsive   B   instinctive   C   intuitive   D   intensive
E   illusive

30   The high _____ of road accidents on the motorway is giving cause for
serious concern.
A   occurrence   B   occasion   C   incident   D   incidence
E   coincidence

31   I've _____ my keys, have you seen them anywhere?
A   misplaced   B   mislaid   C   mistaken   D   missed
E   misappropriated

32   The _____ of the Annual General Meeting were taken by the Company
Secretary.
A   reports   B   points   C   discussions   D   minutes
E   resolutions

33   The cliffs on this part of the coast are constantly being _____ by the sea.
A   impaired   B   rubbed   C   decomposed   D   erupted
E   eroded

34   In your criticism of this writer's work, I think you have done less than
     _____ to the elegance of his style.
     A   justice   B   approval   C   honour   D   appreciation
     E   praise

35   The scarcity of housing accommodation means that people can no longer
     afford to _____ where they live.
     A   look and see   B   come and go   C   pick and choose
     D   stop and start   E   buy and sell

36   The essayist, William Hazlitt, was one of the most distinguished men of
     _____ of his time.
     A   letters   B   books   C   writings   D   papers   E   publications

37   The island where these rare birds nest has been declared a _____ area.
     A   conservative   B   conservation   C   preservative
     D   preservation   E   protective

38   It is absolutely _____ for the Manager to see this report without delay.
     A   insistent   B   inescapable   C   important   D   imperative
     E   incumbent

39   Mrs Parsons has had the couch in her sitting-room _____ in red velvet.
     A   sewn   B   dressed   C   upholstered   D   enriched
     E   clothed

40   I can't quite make out the _____ at the bottom of this manuscript.
     A   signing   B   signature   C   subscription   D   signal
     E   significance

Section B

After each of the passages in this section, there are a number of questions or
unfinished statements about the passage, each with four suggested answers.
Choose the one you think best. **Give one answer only** to each question. Read
each passage right through before choosing your answer.

First Passage

Visitors to St Paul's Cathedral are sometimes astonished as they walk round
the space under the dome to come upon a statue which would appear to be that
of a retired gladiator meditating upon a wasted life. They are still more
astonished when they see under it an inscription indicating that it represents
5 the English writer, Samuel Johnson. The statue is by Bacon, but it is not one of
his best works. The figure is, as often in eighteenth-century sculpture, clothed
only in a loose robe which leaves arms, legs and one shoulder bare. But the
strangeness for us is not one of costume only. If we know anything of Johnson,
we know that he was constantly ill all through his life; and whether we know
10 anything of him or not we are apt to think of a literary man as a delicate, weakly,
nervous sort of person. Nothing can be further from that than the muscular
statue. And in this matter the statue is perfectly right. And the fact which it
reports is far from being unimportant. The body and the mind are inextricably
interwoven in all of us, and certainly in Johnson's case the influence of the body
15 was obvious and conspicuous. His melancholy, his constantly repeated convic-

tion of the general unhappiness of human life, was certainly the result of his constitutional infirmities. On the other hand, his courage, and his entire indifference to pain, were partly due to his great bodily strength. Perhaps the vein of rudeness, almost of fierceness, which sometimes showed itself in his conversa-
20 tion, was the natural temper of an invalid and suffering giant. That at any rate is what he was. He was the victim from childhood of a disease which resembled St Vitus's Dance. He never knew the natural joy of a free and vigorous use of his limbs; when he walked it was like the struggling walk of one in irons. All accounts agree that his strange gesticulations and contortions were painful for
25 his friends to witness and attracted crowds of starers in the streets. But Reynolds says that he could sit still for his portrait to be taken, and that when his mind was engaged by a conversation the convulsions ceased. In any case, it is certain that neither this perpetual misery, nor his constant fear of losing his reason, nor his many grave attacks of illness, ever induced him to surrender the privileges
30 that belonged to his physical strength. He justly thought no character so disagreeable as that of a chronic invalid, and was determined not to be one himself. He had known what it was to live on fourpence a day and scorned the life of sofa cushions and tea into which well-attended old gentlemen so easily slip.

41 Visitors to St Paul's Cathedral are surprised when they look at Johnson's statue because

A they don't expect it to be there
B it's dressed in Roman costume
C it's situated in the dome
D it's dressed in eighteenth-century costume

42 We understand from the passage that most eighteenth-century sculpture was

A done by a man called Bacon
B not very well made
C loosely draped
D left bare

43 What is the writer's general opinion about literary men?

A they have well-developed muscles
B they suffer from nervous breakdowns
C they have weak intellects
D they suffer from poor health

44 "The body and the mind are inextricably interwoven" means

A they have little effect on each other
B they are confused by all of us
C they interact with each other
D they are mixed up in all of us

45 Johnson's unhappiness was caused by

A his melancholy nature
B his physical disabilities
C his strength of character
D his ill-temper

46   The disease that Johnson had to endure made him

    A   very irascible
    B   want to dance
    C   very talkative
    D   grow very large

47   The author says Johnson found it very difficult to walk because

    A   he couldn't control his legs
    B   he generally wore irons round his legs
    C   people always stared at him
    D   it hurt his friends to watch him

48   Reynolds stated that when Johnson was being painted he was able to

    A   talk freely
    B   think clearly
    C   stop moving
    D   move comfortably

49   Because Johnson was very strong physically he could

    A   expect to become insane
    B   endure a lot of pain
    C   claim certain benefits
    D   experience great unhappiness

50   According to the passage, Johnson had

    A   never had enough money to live on
    B   managed to live on tea only
    C   lived frugally in the past
    D   always lived in easy circumstances

Second Passage

    But the most memorable day for Laura was that on which the Bishop came
to consecrate an extension of the churchyard and walked round it in his long
robes, with a cross carried before him and a book in his hands, and the clergy
of the district following. The schoolchildren, wearing their best clothes, were
5 drawn up to watch. "It makes a nice change from school," somebody said, but
to Laura the ceremony was but a prelude.
    She had lingered after the other children had gone home, and the school-
mistress, who, after all, had not been invited to the vicarage to tea as she had
hoped, took her round the churchyard and told her all she knew of its history
10 and architecture, then took her home to tea.
    A small, two-roomed cottage adjoined the school and was provided for the
schoolmistress; this the school managers had furnished in the manner they
thought suitable for one of her degree. "Very comfortable" they had stated in
their advertisement; but to a new tenant it must have looked very bare. The
15 downstairs room had a table for meals, four cane-bottomed chairs, a white
marble-topped sideboard stood for luxury and a wicker armchair by the fireplace for comfort. The tiled floor was partly covered with brown matting.
    But Miss Shepherd was "artistic" and by the time Laura saw the room a
transformation had taken place. A green cloth with bobble fringe hid the

20 nakedness of the centre table; the backs of the cane chairs were draped with
white crocheted lace, tied with blue bows, and the wicker chairs were cushioned.
The walls were so crowded with pictures, photographs, Japanese fans, wool-
work letter-racks, hanging pincushions, and other trophies of the present
tenant's skill that, as the children used to say: "You couldn't so much as stick
25 a pin in."

"Don't you think I've made it nice and cosy, dear?" said Miss Shepherd, after
Laura had been shown and duly admired each specimen of her handiwork, and
Laura heartily agreed, for it seemed to her the very height of elegance.

It was her first invitation to grown-up tea, with biscuits and jam – not spread
30 on her bread for her, as at home, but spooned on to her plate by herself and
spread exactly as she had seen her father spread his. After tea, Miss Shepherd
played the piano and showed Laura her photographs and books, finally pre-
senting her with one and walking part of the way home with her. How thrilled
Laura was when, at their parting, she said: "Well, I think we have had quite a
35 nice little time, after all, Laura."

At the time of that tea-drinking, Laura must have been eleven or twelve, one
of Miss Shepherd's "big girls" and a person to be trusted, but that rare invitation
to tea was never repeated.

51   The Bishop had come to the village to

   A   see the church
   B   visit the clergy
   C   walk round the churchyard
   D   bless part of the churchyard

52   For Laura, we understand that attending the ceremony was

   A   better than going to school
   B   the nicest thing she'd ever done
   C   the beginning of a lovely day
   D   her only chance to wear good clothes

53   Laura didn't leave with the other children because she

   A   wasn't in any hurry
   B   wanted to see round the church
   C   hoped to go to tea at the vicarage
   D   expected to go to tea with the schoolmistress

54   It seems that originally the schoolmistress's cottage was

   A   ill-furnished
   B   plainly furnished
   C   luxuriously furnished
   D   comfortably furnished

55   Because Miss Shepherd was artistic she had improved the cottage by

   A   painting the walls
   B   hanging paintings on the walls
   C   sticking pins in the walls
   D   draping lace on the walls

56   What is meant by "other trophies of the present tenant's skill"?

   A   cups and prizes won by Miss Shepherd
   B   animal heads shot by Miss Shepherd
   C   various things made by Miss Shepherd
   D   works of art made by Miss Shepherd

57   From the passage we understand that the overall effect of the cottage was

   A   elegant
   B   bleak
   C   artful
   D   fussy

58   Laura was particularly pleased at having tea with the schoolmistress because

   A   she was allowed to have jam on her biscuits
   B   she was allowed to eat jam with the spoon
   C   it was assumed she could play the piano
   D   it was assumed she would behave correctly

59   Why did Miss Shepherd use the words "after all" when saying good-bye to Laura?

   A   she was surprised Laura had enjoyed herself
   B   she hadn't expected to enjoy herself again
   C   she had been disappointed that day
   D   everything had gone wrong that day

60   The main theme of the passage is

   A   the importance of the Bishop's visit
   B   a wonderful day in Laura's life
   C   an unexciting invitation to tea
   D   the pleasure of a day off school

PAPER 3: USE OF ENGLISH (3 hours)

SECTION A

1. Fill each of the numbered blanks in the following passage with **one** suitable word.

Outwardly you may be on friendly terms with the people next door, but, if

the truth _____(1) known, you do not think much of them. Their

ways may be _____(2) enough, but they are not your ways. It is not

hatred, far _____(3) envy; neither is it contempt exactly. Only you do not understand why they live as they _____(4). You _____(5)

people by _____(6) social background. They were not brought

up as you were – not that they are to blame for that, but certain advantages

that you had were _____(7) them. Rude noises come from that house

next door that you would not _____(8) from respectable people.

Laughter late _____(9) night, when you want to sleep – how coarse

it _____(10)! Then there is that young woman who sings! What

voices the people next door always have, and what a _____(11) of

songs! Why do they never try a new one? There _____(12) be new

songs from time to time but you never hear them next door. Years after a song

is _____(13) it goes on next door. A popular song never dies. The

people next door rescue it after it has been hounded off the street and warm it

into _____(14) life. And so it goes. Everything they do shows just

what sort of people they are. _____(15) at the things they hang out

in their garden. If your things looked like that you would at _____(16)

keep them indoors. It is not that they are so old, but they were chosen with

_____(17) monstrously bad _____(18) in the first place.

What in the world do people want to _____(19) a house with things

like that for? They must have cost enough, too, and for that amount of money

they could have bought – but what is the _____(20) of talking? There

are distinctions that you never can make people feel.

2. Finish each of the following sentences in such a way that it means exactly the same as the sentence printed before it.

Example: They say that Shakespeare wrote this sonnet

Answer: This sonnet *is said to have been written by Shakespeare*

It seems likely that my brother will get the job he is after.

1 There is every ....

Is this the only red sweater you have in stock?

2 Haven't you ....

They were talking very earnestly when I saw them in the corridor.

3 They were deep ....

I don't believe he intends to do any more business with your firm.

4 It is my ....

John's attitude to his wife has always puzzled me.

5 I have ....

This is the last time I shall ever try to learn to ski.

6 I shall ....

I can't remember where you said the Browns lived.

7 Where ....

Would Saturday, August 9th, be convenient for Mr Jones?

8 Could Mr Jones ....?

I think it would be better not to give him your address.

9 I don't ....

No one in the college knows as much about students' problems as Mr Harvey.

10 Mr Harvey ....

3. Fill each of the numbered blanks with a suitable word or phrase.

Example
      Susan: How much did Harry pay for his new house?
      Mary: Over £12,000.
      Susan: Oh, so it *cost him* over £12,000.

1   Whatever reasons he had given me, I .... believed him.

2   By the end of April Peter .... in England for six months.

3   They ....to come to the wedding, if they had known in time.

4   The earliest remains of primitive man are said .... in Central Africa.

5   "I don't suppose I .... to Paris again next year."

6   "Don't forget to turn out the lights in the sitting-room."
    "All right! That's the second time ...."

7   "You might have dusted the furniture before Aunt Maud came."
    "How .... today?"

8   "I don't much like the way you've cooked this fish."
    "Well, next time .... then!"

9   "Excuse me, but .... to put the milk in the fridge?"

10   "Veronica said she wasn't going to tell her mother about her engagement, but she did."
    "Oh, so .... after all?"

4. For each of the sentences below, write a new sentence **as similar as possible in meaning to the original sentence,** but using the word given in capital letters.

Example: How fast can your car go?
      SPEED

Answer: *What speed can your car do?*

1   There's no need to telephone me when you get to London.
    BOTHER

....

2 She will not be going to America this year on any account.
   QUESTION

....

3 John's train will probably be delayed because of the fog.
   LIKELY

....

4 Why wouldn't you answer my question about Jane?
   REFUSE

....

5 The garden is too small for a swimming pool.
   ROOM

....

6 We could have walked to the station, it was so near.
   ENOUGH

....

7 It is just possible to catch the bus if we hurry.
   MIGHT

....

8 He is easy to understand because he has a very clear voice.
   DISTINCTLY

....

9 Did he say why he hadn't telephoned?
   REASON

....

10 I don't mind listening to Pop, but classical music is my favourite.
    BEST

....

SECTION B

5. Read the following passage, and then answer the questions which follow it.

The technological revolution in education has taken an unconscionable time in arriving. It was in the last decade that programmed learning, springing from the laboratories of Harvard and California, gave the promise of self-spaced, continually assessed instruction that carried with it its own remedial teaching. There
5 were dark prophecies of children being plugged-in to machines that would turn

out wan, limp degrees at the other end, endlessly regurgitating their force-fed knowledge like Professor Skinner's pigeons, which had been taught to play table tennis by the same process. There were jokes about language laboratories, with their serried rows of headphones, glass booths and switches; many teachers felt like disc-jockeys when operating them. The use of film was being rediscovered through the medium of television. Film slides came into vogue, followed soon after by the closed-loop film, which could be seen over and over again, stopped and discussed, or wound back at the touch of a button.

Any one of these teaching aids was capable of adding to the learning process, but it was their combination that brought out the enthusiasm and allowed us to talk of a "technology of education." As the jargon had it, it was the "man-machine interaction" that ought to have provided the excitement. But somehow, it never turned out that way. Instead, we seem to be moving crabwise into the new era; hesitant with uncertainty, but changing, irreversibly, the technique of classroom teaching as we go.

Time has removed the merely fashionable, and proved the virtues of others. No school now would be without its overhead projector or its tape recorder. The language laboratory has found its place; not perhaps, an indispensable tool, but superb for the short, intensive oral drills that used to result in utter boredom as the teacher went round the class hearing the students individually.

Television for schools has arrived, after an uphill battle. There are still not as many sets around as there should be, but the Education Authority's service, linking hundreds of schools and colleges and providing local material and video-tape recordings, has given it a new importance.

Yet TV has other uses, such as projecting a microscopic image to an entire class, or broadcasting the excellent national services relayed by the broadcasting companies, or, as a mirror, looking into a classroom to study teaching techniques. All these uses are now firmly established in the schools and colleges, and a new generation of teachers, armed with techniques and familiarity with the cameras, are more likely to insist upon their creative use.

In time, a newcomer on the horizon may make even TV look like a passing fashion. This is EVR, or electronic video recording. The point about this technique is that it turns a standard TV receiver into a potent moving-picture book, whose pages can be turned, stopped, or moved back. By using an attachment to the TV set, the screen can show prerecorded material, old prints, pages of books, stills, maps or a variety of other material. The costs of this equipment will, on a rental basis, bring recorded lectures and other teaching material within the range of each school, and it will eventually prove very attractive.

There are other, more traditional aids, which have already won acceptance. There is the film; there is, we ought not to forget, chalk and talk; and there is – all-enduring – the book.

Finally, and just for the record, there is one other potential candidate – computer-based instruction, a form of teaching which might have theoretical potential but which, in practical terms, is a non-starter as far as current financial and technical resources are concerned.

1 Where did programmed learning originate and what was its main purpose?

....

....

2   What was unusual about Professor Skinner's pigeons? ....

....

3   What was the advantage of using closed-loop film? ....

....

4   Being able to talk about a "technology of education" was brought about by

....

....

5   How is the technique of classroom teaching changing? ....

....

6   When was the "last decade"? (l. 2)..

7   "carried with it" (l. 4) refers to ....

8   How would the meaning of the sentence (l. 5) be altered if the words
    "dark prophecies of" were not there? ....

....

9   To what does the phrase "by the same process" (l. 8) refer? ....

....

10 What is the meaning of "came into vogue"? (l. 11) ....

11 What should have provided "the excitement"? (l. 17) ....

....

12 Why does the writer use the phrase "moving crabwise"? (l. 18) ....

....

13 Which technical aids have been proved to have virtues? ....

....

14 How does the use of a language laboratory help the teacher? ....

....

15 It will be possible for all schools to have EVR in the future because ....

....

16   "all-enduring" (l. 46) with reference to the book means ....

....

17   Why does the author think "computer-based instruction" (l. 48) is not
     widely used at present? ....

18   In a paragraph of not more than 100 words describe some of the new
     "technology of education" as contrasted with "more traditional aids".

....

....

....

....

....

....

....

....

....

....

SECTION C

6. You are anxious to let your flat and have inserted the following advertisement
in the accommodation column of an evening newspaper.

> A lux. s/c sgl. furn. gdn. flt.
> 1 rm., k & b. C.H. Cpts., Col. T.V., tel., fridge, ckr., h/c.
> £120 p.m. Refs. rqd.
> Avail. mid. Apr.
> Tel: 01-542-6070 Evgs after 6.

Write a telephone conversation between yourself and an interested caller in
which you give full details of the flat. The dialogue should not be more than
150 words.

PAPER 4: LISTENING COMPREHENSION (40 minutes)

The passages on which these questions are based will be found in the Appendix.

First Passage

1   What was Anderson's first impression of the room?

A   He felt he had always wanted to live there
B   He knew he had to live there some time
C   He knew he had lived there before
D   He felt as if he had always lived there

2   The woman asked Anderson to wait because

A   he was too early for his appointment
B   she had to go and confirm his appointment
C   her brother had told her to keep Anderson waiting
D   her brother had to be advised of Anderson's arrival

3   From the information given in the text, how could the room best be described?

A   gloomy and seldom used
B   dusty and seldom used
C   dark and overcrowded
D   dark with musty curtains

4   From the passage we understand that Anderson had come to the house in the first place because

A   he was interested in buying a house
B   he thought the house might be for sale
C   he was looking for a house to sell
D   he wanted to sell his own house

5   What was the forcible sensation that struck Anderson while he was waiting in the room? He felt

A   he had been converted
B   he was a stranger to himself
C   he was a displaced person
D   he had been disembodied

Second Passage

6 From the passage it would seem that the writer

A is unsympathetic to drop-outs
B believes we are living in a sick society
C is attracted by unhappy people
D finds pleasure in other people's eccentricities

7 Why do you think it is often difficult for the bank clerk to enjoy the sort of breakfast he likes?

A there is no sun in England
B the English weather is unpredictable
C the sun in England is not strong enough to toast bread
D he doesn't like bread toasted on both sides

8 The couple the writer refers to decided to live in a tree because

A they believed they were apes
B it made them more respected
C they believed it was their natural habitat
D they thought houses were only for animals

9 What do we learn from the text about the secretary who collected earwigs?

A she never neglected her work
B she never stopped working
C she wasted time looking after the earwigs
D she only kept earwigs in her desk

10 From the information given what impression do we receive of the writer's character?

A he has no personality
B he is mildly eccentric
C he is rather intolerant
D he is very ordinary

Third Passage

11 What was unusual about the old man travelling in a first class carriage?

A he wasn't wearing the right clothes
B he was eating a very big lunch
C he didn't look very democratic
D he didn't look as if he ate much

12 The old man implied that tourists

A weren't welcomed in Treliss
B were overwhelmed in Treliss
C had driven him to Treliss
D had driven him through Treliss

13 Why did the old man think Americans should pay a tax in England?

A they didn't speak English properly
B they brought too much equipment with them
C they caused a lot of damage in the countryside
D they caused a lot of irritation by their presence

14 The old man did not think Harkness was an American because

A he had never lived in England
B he had never lived in America
C he didn't look like one
D he didn't sound like one

15 According to the passage the old man made Harkness

A feel happy
B want to smile
C act violently
D feel fed up

Fourth Passage

16 Shoreditch is interesting because of its

A municipal authority
B Jacobean architecture
C theatrical associations
D religious buildings

17 Why was it difficult to perform plays in seventeenth century London?

A there weren't enough actors
B there weren't enough theatres
C the church didn't allow it
D the city government didn't allow it

18 What was one of the particularly interesting things that Richard Burbage did?

A he erected the Globe Theatre
B he only acted the role of Hamlet
C he built the Shoreditch Theatre
D he acted all the characters in Shakespeare

19 The Curtain Theatre was so-called because

A there were curtains hanging round the auditorium
B there was a curtain in front of the audience
C it was built on the corner of Curtain Road
D it was built on the Curtain Road factory site

20 William Shakespeare was chiefly employed at the Curtain as

A a family butcher
B an original playwright
C an adaptor of plays
D an actor of principal parts

PAPER 5: INTERVIEW (12 minutes)

Section A *Photograph*

Look at this photograph carefully and be prepared to answer some questions about it.

Describe the scene in the photograph.

Would you consider such a place pleasant or unpleasant for children?

Would you consider it safe for children to play here unsupervised?

Do you think children should be allowed to run on the grass and jump on the statues in parks?

Importance of open spaces in towns and cities.

Necessity of providing somewhere for children to play.

Parks and gardens – provision in candidate's country.

Art as a stimulant to children's imagination.

Section B *Topics*

Choose one of the following topics and prepare to give your views on it, for
1½ to 2 minutes. You may make notes but do not write out a full speech.

1   The problem of noise in modern society.

2   The value of the arts in developing personality.

3   The case for state-owned housing.

Section C *Dialogue*

(Prepare yourself to read the part of MASTERS. The teacher will read the
other part.)

MASTERS: I see Simpson has got that job as Area Manager.

Allen: I thought he would.

MASTERS: So did I. It's funny, isn't it, how someone like that always seems
to get the plum jobs – I mean, the sort of person you or I wouldn't
be taken in by for a moment. Simpson's not particularly intelligent and certainly not nearly so well qualified as I am myself, and
I happen to know he's been involved in one or two rather shady
deals on the side. Yet, in two years, he's edged his way up from
the bottom and before we know where we are, he's posing as a
pillar of the Establishment.

Allen: It's probably no more than a question of being in the right place
at the right time.

MASTERS: It's more than that. It's an inborn instinct for self-advancement.
I only wish I had it.

Allen: You and I were born naturally lazy, I expect.

MASTERS: Oh, Simpson's not lazy, I'll grant you that, but then I wouldn't
agree that you and I are either. No, it's just the way he has of
insinuating himself into everyone's confidence that I object to –
that slimy way of talking as if he were doing you a favour when
all the time he's working out some way to give you a dig in the
back.

Allen: From the way you're talking anyone would think you didn't like
him.

MASTERS: Like him? I loathe him, he revolts me. Always has, ever since he
stole the liquorice allsorts out of my locker at school.

Section D *Situations*

1   You are at the railway station. Go to the Booking Office and enquire about the times of an excursion to York and the fare.

2   Your eyes have been troubling you. Ask the oculist for his advice.

3   You are just going to bed one night when a friend arrives at your flat with a suitcase. What do you say?

4   You are expecting a parcel from abroad which hasn't arrived. Go to the Post Office and enquire about it.

5   You are having a noisy party at home when your neighbour telephones to complain. Apologise and explain.

TEST THREE

Answer questions 1, 2 and 3. You should spend about the same amount of time on each.

Section A

1. Either (*a*) Humour – describe the kind of situations that make you laugh.

or (*b*) A street market – its atmosphere, bustle and colour.

2. Either (*a*) Discuss the problem of violence in modern society and say how you think it should be dealt with.

or (*b*) Give your opinion of the influence of TV and the advertising media on public opinion.

Section B

3. Read the following passage, and then answer the questions which follow it.

To be properly enjoyed, a walking tour should be gone upon alone. If you go in a company, or even in pairs, it is no longer a walking tour in anything but name; it is something else and more in the nature of a picnic. A walking tour should be gone upon alone, because you should be able to stop and go on, and
5 follow this way and that, as the whim takes you; and because you must have your own pace, and neither trot alongside a champion walker, nor mince in time with a girl. And you must be open to all impressions and let your thoughts take colour from what you see. You should be as a pipe for any wind to play upon. There should be no cackle of voices at your elbow, to jar on the meditative
10 silence of the morning. And so long as a man is reasoning he cannot surrender himself to that fine intoxication that comes of much motion in the open air, that begins in a sort of dazzle and sluggishness of the brain, and ends in a peace that passes comprehension.
During the first day or so of any tour there are moments of bitterness, when
15 the traveller feels more than coldly towards his knapsack, when he is half in a mind to throw it bodily over the hedge. Yet it soon acquires a property of easiness. It becomes magnetic; the spirit of the journey enters into it. And no sooner have you passed the straps over your shoulder again than the lees of sleep are cleared from you, you pull yourself together with a shake and fall at once into
20 your stride. And surely, of all possible moods, this, in which a man takes the road, is the best.

(*a*) Comment on the writer's use of the expression "in anything but name". (ll. 2–3)

(*b*) What in the opinion of the writer are the main disadvantages of having company on a walking tour?

(*c*) "You should be as a pipe for any wind to play on." (l. 8)
What is the significance of this statement?

(*d*) How, according to the writer, is man affected by prolonged walking in the open air?

(*e*) What impression do we receive from the use of the word "bodily"? (l. 16)

(*f*) The writer describes the knapsack as becoming magnetic. In what way is this an accurate description?

(*g*) Taking the theme as a whole, what do you think is "the spirit of the journey" referred to? (l. 17)

PAPER 2: READING COMPREHENSION (1¼ hours)

Section A

Choose the word or phrase which best completes each sentence. **Give one answer only** to each question.

1 The painting in the long gallery is _____ to Rembrandt.
A prescribed B attributed C attached D assigned
E referred

2 Maria _____ missed the first train so as to travel on the same one as John.
A deliberately B intensively C decisively D objectively
E predictably

3 You will find the reference to Darwin's theory of evolution in _____ two of the Encyclopaedia.
A tome B serial C volume D pamphlet E treatise

4 Fortunately for the Police, the demonstration turned out to be quite _____.
A peacemaking B passive C pastoral D peaceful
E pacific

5 If John hadn't tried to stand up in the boat, he wouldn't have fallen _____ into the lake.
A top to toe B head over heels C back to back
D shoulder to shoulder E neck and neck

6 When it saw the dog by the water, the heron _____ its wings and rose into the air.
A flipped B flicked C flapped D folded E furled

7   In the orchestra the oboe and the bassoon are two of the _____ instruments.
    A   breath   B   wind   C   throat   D   mouth   E   lip

8   Professor Jordan is well known for his _____ into the habits of the common
    house-fly.
    A   examination   B   exposition   C   theory   D   research
    E   deposition

9   I was unable to pay all my electricity bill at once, so I sent half the
    amount _____.
    A   on account   B   in advance   C   by degrees   D   in credit
    E   in settlement

10 He's a very _____ man, he always says exactly what he means.
    A   dull   B   observant   C   obtuse   D   blunt   E   keen

11 The twins are so alike, it is impossible to _____ them apart.
    A   discern   B   tell   C   discover   D   divide   E   decide

12 The patient was found to be suffering from _____ injuries as a result of
    his fall.
    A   multiplied   B   multiple   C   multifarious   D   multitudinous
    E   multipliable

13 Alan has not seen his brother for ten years and has no idea of his _____.
    A   living   B   place   C   residence   D   address   E   destination

14 Our Art teacher has applied for a year's _____ leave to study in Paris.
    A   sabbatical   B   suspended   C   satanic   D   sustained
    E   superfluous

15 There is something wrong with the dining room clock, it only goes _____.
    A   in bits and pieces   B   by hook or by crook
    C   by leaps and bounds   D   in twos and threes
    E   in fits and starts

16 Sitting by the lake, we could hear the _____ of the sheep on the hills
    behind us.
    A   bawling   B   buzzing   C   bleating   D   barking   E   braying

17 "I'm sure there are spiders in this room," said Mary, "look at those _____
    in the corner."
    A   cobwebs   B   networks   C   fillets   D   meshes   E   filaments

18 My little niece is not allowed to play with the children next door because
    one of them is suffering from a _____ disease.
    A   contiguous   B   concentrated   C   contagious   D   touching
    E   transmitting

19 Arrogance and pride are similar in meaning, but there is _____ difference
    between them.
    A   a submerged   B   an indecisive   C   an indistinct   D   a subtle
    E   a subconscious

20 The sky looks so _____ that I am afraid there is going to be a storm.
    A   overcast   B   overdone   C   overshadowed   D   overburdened
    E   overwhelmed

21 If you want to slim, you should avoid eating _____ foods such as bread and potatoes.
    A fatty   B starchy   C greasy   D sugary   E spicy

22 Morphia is sometimes used _____ severe pain.
    A to stifle   B to suffocate   C to smother   D to deaden
    E to decimate

23 I have it on very good _____ that Mr Jones will be retiring in September.
    A reference   B authority   C information   D inference
    E authorisation

24 The young man who was arrested for dangerous driving was _____ with a caution by the magistrate.
    A let off   B sent down   C put out   D given up
    E turned in

25 He lost his temper and _____ his teeth in rage.
    A bit   B ground   C curled   D rasped   E rattled

26 I wish I could get out of the habit of _____ when I feel embarrassed.
    A blooming   B firing   C rouging   D flaming   E blushing

27 As a pianist his _____ is brilliant, but I don't care much for his interpretation.
    A technique   B technicality   C technology   D exhibitionism
    E mastery

28 What do you think of this old teapot? I bought it at our village _____ sale.
    A rubbish   B rubble   C refuse   D jumble   E deposit

29 We arrived at the theatre only two minutes before the curtain _____.
    A rose up   B went up   C got up   D lifted up   E came up

30 My boss must be the most _____ man in the world. He is so obstinate.
    A pigheaded   B featherheaded   C lightheaded
    D hardheaded   E softheaded

31 The noise outside the hotel at night is hardly _____ to a good night's sleep.
    A considerate   B conducive   C consistent   D conformable
    E conclusive

32 In spite of the thunderstorm, the children slept _____ all night.
    A noisily   B soundly   C roundly   D resonantly
    E densely

33 Camilla is very _____, she is always buying clothes she cannot really afford.
    A expensive   B exorbitant   C extravagant   D exuberant
    E extrovert

34 The tweed for this suit _____ in Scotland.
    A was knitted   B was threaded   C was laced
    D was crocheted   E was woven

35 The cat jumped on the table and began _____ the milk from the jug.
    A to lap   B to suck   C to spoon   D to siphon   E to strain

36   After searching for half an hour, the children found their ball in the _____
     by the lilac bushes.
     A   underground   B   underworld   C   undergrowth
     D   underpass   E   undertow

37   Before my grandfather died, he made _____ for all his children in his will.
     A   protection   B   provision   C   disposition   D   attachment
     E   disposal

38   The Prime Minister's broadcast _____ the terms of entry to the Common
     Market.
     A   cleared   B   expressed   C   enunciated   D   enlightened
     E   clarified

39   The name of the hotel is _____. I wish I could remember it.
     A   on the tip of my tongue   B   at my finger tips
     C   in the palm of my hand   D   in front of my nose
     E   at arm's length

40   The present Parliament will _____ on the 8th September, prior to the
     General Election.
     A   be destroyed   B   be decomposed   C   be dissolved
     D   be discontinued   E   be disconnected

Section B

In this section you will find after each of the passages a number of questions
or unfinished statements. Choose the one you think fits best. **Give one answer
only** to each question. Read each passage right through before choosing your
answer.

First Passage

The Fore and Fit Regiment had enjoyed unbroken peace for five days, and
were beginning, in spite of dysentery, to recover their nerve. But they were not
happy, for they did not know the work in hand, and had they known, would
not have known how to do it. Throughout those five days with no old soldiers
5 who might have taught them the craft of the game, they discussed together their
misadventures in the past – how one of their regiment had been alive at dawn
and dead before dusk and with what shrieks and struggles another one had given
up his soul. Death was a new and horrible thing to the sons of mechanics who
were used to dying decently in their beds; and their careful conservation in
10 barracks had done nothing to make them look upon it with less dread.
     Very early in the dawn the bugles began to blow, and the Fore and Fit, filled
with a misguided enthusiasm, turned out without waiting for a cup of coffee and
a biscuit; and were rewarded by being kept waiting in the cold while the other
regiments leisurely prepared for the battle.
15   The Fore and Fit waited, leaning upon their rifles and listening to the protests
of their empty stomachs. The Colonel did his best to remedy the situation as
soon as it was borne in upon him that the affair would not begin at once, and so
well did he succeed that the coffee was just ready when – the men moved off,
their Band leading. Even then there had been a mistake in the time, and the Fore
20 and Fit came out into the valley ten minutes before the proper hour. Their Band

wheeled to the right after reaching the open, and retired behind a little rocky knoll, still playing while the Regiment went past.

It was not a pleasant sight that opened on the unobstructed view, for the lower end of the valley appeared to be filled by a vast army in position – real and
25 actual regiments, and – of this there was no doubt – firing bullets which cut up the ground a hundred yards in front of the leading company. Over that bullet-marked ground the Regiment had to pass. Being half capable of thinking for itself, it fired a volley by the simple process of putting its rifle to its shoulder and pulling the trigger. The bullets may have accounted for some of the watchers on
30 the hillside, but they certainly did not affect the mass of enemy in front, while the noise of the bullets drowned any orders that might have been given.

The Fore and Fit continued to go forward, but with shortened stride. Where were the other regiments? They took open order instinctively, lying down and firing at random, rushing a few paces forward and lying down again, according
35 to the regulations. Once in this formation, each man felt himself desperately alone, and edged in towards his fellow for comfort's sake.

Then the crack of his neighbour's rifle at his ear led him to fire as rapidly as he could, again for the sake of the comfort of the noise. The reward was not long delayed. Five volleys plunged the soldiers in banked smoke impenetrable to the
40 eye, and the bullets began to hit the ground twenty or thirty yards in front of the firers, as the weight of the loaded guns dragged down and to the right arms wearied with holding the kick of the jolting rifles. The Company Commanders peered helplessly through the smoke, the more nervous mechanically trying to fan it away with their helmets.
45 "High and to the left!" shouted a Captain till he was hoarse. "No good! Cease firing, and let it drift away a bit."

Three and four times the bugles shrieked the order, and when it was obeyed the Fore and Fit looked expecting to see the enemy lying before them cut down by the bullets, but a light wind drove the smoke away and showed the enemy
50 still in position and apparently unaffected.

41   Why were the Fore and Fit Regiment feeling uneasy?

A   they were recovering from an illness
B   they had lost their nerve
C   they didn't know what to expect
D   they didn't know how to work

42   The soldiers knew very little about fighting because

A   they didn't listen to what they were told
B   there was nobody experienced to tell them
C   they had made many mistakes in the past
D   there was very little time to learn

43   What effect had being made to stay in barracks had upon them?

A   it made them afraid of dying
B   it made them thoughtless about dying
C   it made them prepared for death
D   it made them face death unafraid

44   Why did the men of the Fore and Fit choose to forego their breakfast?

    A   they were too frightened to eat
    B   there was only coffee and biscuits
    C   they didn't have time to eat
    D   they were too eager to fight

45   The colonel tried to get some food and drink for the men because

    A   he could hear the soldiers' stomachs rumbling
    B   he liked to resolve difficult situations
    C   he realised the fighting would not start immediately
    D   he could hear the soldiers protesting

46   Why were the Regiment apprehensive about moving along the valley?

    A   they were unable to judge their distance from the enemy
    B   they were unable to see clearly as the view was obstructed
    C   they appeared to be greatly outnumbered by the enemy
    D   the ground had been eroded in front of them

47   The soldiers of the Fore and Fit began to fire their rifles because

    A   they were ordered to
    B   they were trained to
    C   they were in the right position
    D   they were good shots

48   Because the men in the Regiment felt alone when fighting they

    A   closed ranks
    B   fired quicker
    C   ran forward
    D   lay down

49   What made the soldiers' arms so tired?

    A   holding up the guns
    B   loading the guns
    C   the weight of the guns
    D   the recoil of the guns

50   Which of the following best explains "cut down"? (l. 48)

    A   slaughtered
    B   executed
    C   impaled
    D   decapitated

Second Passage

    The wickedest elephant I ever knew was called Taw Sin Ma (Miss Wild Elephant). I never knew her when she was a calf, but she cannot have been greatly loved, to have earned herself a name like that. She was about twenty-five years old when I first knew her, and there was nothing in her recorded history which
5 gave any explanation of why she should hate every European she saw.
    She recognised a European by his appearance quite as much as by smell,

because she would attack a Burman if he were wearing a khaki shirt. I had a nasty experience with her, when she first attacked me on sight, and then chased me, following my trail by scent for four miles. It was terrifying.

0   I met her by chance, when I was walking from one camp to another. We came on her suddenly, and she went for us at once. The Burman I had with me stampeded in one direction, and I in another, and for two miles I was not sure whether I was on the right track back to the camp I had left. There would have been no hope for me if she had caught up with me, unless I had found refuge up

5 a tree. But I knew well that if I had done that I might have had to stay there for twenty-four hours or longer. As she was hunting by scent my pace was a little faster than hers. She wore a brass danger bell around her neck, the docile elephants wore wooden bells. Often it sounded from the bell as though she were nearly up to me, at times as though she had cut me off. Of course, I know that

20 sounds in the jungle are deceptive, and play tricks; but it was not pleasant. This experience gave me the first opportunity I had ever had of trying out a trick for delaying a pursuing elephant, by dropping an article of clothing, in the belief that the animal will halt and attack it, and so give one a chance of gaining ground.

25   I first dropped a haversack, but I heard no check in the sound of the clanking bell on the elephant hurrying after me. When I had climbed to the top of the ridge I halted for a few moments, to locate her whereabouts. Then after going as fast as I could along the ridge, I chose the steepest place for my descent, hoping she would hesitate to follow, and there I dropped my khaki shirt, for her to savage,

30 or to chew to her heart's content. But I had no sooner reached the small spur leading to the drainage area below than I heard an avalanche of crashing trees and bamboos, and it needed very little imagination to visualise Taw Sin Ma sitting on her haunches and tobogganing down the sharp incline, much faster than I had done. My shirt had not delayed her for a moment. Perhaps she was

35 holding it in her mouth to chew after she had first caught me. On I plunged, trying to remember to act on the law of the jungle, that one must never hurry and always keep cool. Once one breaks that rule every thorny bush that grows reaches out to impede, to tear and scratch, or even trip one up. I thought of discarding my once white, and very wet vest, but I thought that if I was eventually

40 forced up a tree, I might need something on. My relief was great when I met two men, busy with a crosscut saw on a fallen teak tree. But I had only to shout out the words "Taw Sin Ma" and they joined me in my flight, without asking questions. They soon took the lead, and as I followed I at least had the satisfaction of knowing I was on the right track to camp and to safety.

51   Why was the author unable to discover anything about Taw Sin Ma's hatred of Europeans?

   A   nothing was known about her
   B   she was too old when he knew her
   C   no information was available
   D   she had no recorded history

52   According to the passage the elephant attacked people who

   A   wore khaki shirts
   B   smelt Burmese
   C   looked Burmese
   D   ran away

53   The writer was worried when the elephant was chasing him
     A   because he couldn't climb trees
     B   in case he lost his way
     C   in case he couldn't find the Burman
     D   because time was getting short

54   Why did the author find it difficult to gauge the elephant's position?
     A   she was out of sight
     B   the sound of the bell was unusual
     C   she was out of hearing
     D   the sound conditions were unusual

55   The writer believed that dropping an article of clothing would
     A   encourage an elephant to pursue you
     B   cause an elephant to attack you
     C   hinder an elephant from attacking you
     D   prohibit an elephant from attacking you

56   What made the writer stop at the top of the ridge?
     A   he wanted to place the elephant's position
     B   he wanted to see the best place to descend
     C   he wanted to get his breath back
     D   he wanted to place his own position

57   How was it possible for the writer to guess the whereabouts of Taw Sin Ma?
     A   he could hear her moving in the drainage area
     B   he could hear her masticating his shirt
     C   he could hear the sound of falling timber
     D   he could hear her falling down the slope

58   The elephant came down the slope "sitting on her haunches" is best described as
     A   backsliding down the hill
     B   backing down the hill
     C   coming down the hill backwards
     D   coming down the hill on her backside

59   If a person ignores the law of the jungle the author suggests he will be
     A   hampered
     B   embarrassed
     C   disabled
     D   shackled

60   The writer was pleased to come across the two men in the jungle as they
     A   told him which way to go
     B   knew which way to go
     C   distracted the elephant
     D   ran away from him

PAPER 3: USE OF ENGLISH (3 hours)

SECTION A

1. Fill each of the numbered blanks in the passage with **one** suitable word.

There are a _____(1) many people who _____(2) that elementary teaching might be properly carried _____(3) by teachers provided with only elementary knowledge. _____(4) me assure you that that is the profoundest _____(5) in the world. There is nothing so difficult to do _____(6) to write a good elementary book, and there is nobody so _____(7) to teach properly and well as people who know _____(8) about a subject, and I will tell you _____(9). If I address an audience of people who are occupied in the same _____(10) of business as myself, I can _____(11) that they know a great deal, and that they can find out the blunders I _____(12). If they don't, it is their _____(13) and not mine; but when I appear _____(14) a body of people who know nothing about the _____(15), who take _____(16) gospel whatever I say, _____(17) it becomes necessary for me to consider what I say, to make sure that it will _____(18) examination, and that I do not impose _____(19) the credulity of those who have faith in _____(20).

2. Finish each of the following sentences in such a way that it means exactly the same as the sentence printed before it.

Example: Did he say why he was so late?

Answer: What reason *did he give for being so late*?

He acted very badly in the play last night.

1   He gave ....

I can't think where I left my keys.

2   I have no ....

We never suspected that he was already married.

3   At no time ....

Nothing more can be said about the way Peter behaved.

4   There is ....

Mr Johnson takes that dog with him everywhere.

5   That dog ....

Would it be possible for him to come before Saturday?

6   Is there ....?

Those two sacks of potatoes weigh exactly the same.

7   There is no ....

There is little we can do to help except sympathise.

8   Beyond ....

The Museum is closed this afternoon.

9   There is ....

He answered all my questions very accurately.

10 He gave ....

3. Fill each of the numbered blanks with a suitable word or phrase.

Example:
> **David:** How did you enjoy Rome?
> **Peter:** We never got there. We changed our plans at the last minute.
> **David:** Oh, so you *didn't go to Rome* after all!

1   Do hurry up, Susie, I've .... five minutes.

2 Why doesn't John answer?

He ...., the door's shut.

3 Alexander seems very quiet today. Do you think ....

.... with him?

4 I've got indigestion. I .... that disagreed with me.

5 Is it all right if Mr Samson comes at 4.30?
No, I'm busy then. .... half an hour later.

6 I thought we were going to the Zoo this afternoon.

Oh, really! You know perfectly well .... tomorrow.

7 Excuse me, sir, but a Miss Halliday wants you on the phone.

Oh, tell her .... when I get back from lunch.

8 I do wish you'd take your suit to the cleaners.

Don't fuss. I'll .... on the way to work.

9 Remind me to turn the Television on at eight.
Why?
Because there's a programme .... to see.

10 Mr Jones has had that limp ever since he .... the last War.

4. For each of the following sentences, write a new sentence **as similar as possible in meaning to the original sentence,** but using the word given in capital letters.

Example: Do you know where you are going for your holidays yet?
DECISION

Answer: *Have you made any decision about where you're going for your holidays yet?*

1 I shall be unable to keep my appointment with Mr Higgs.
CANCEL

....

2 If I'd been Mary, I wouldn't have told John about the car accident.
PLACE

....

3   The stories Michael tells about his war experiences are quite incredible.
    BEYOND

    ....

4   It's no use asking Mrs Simpson to sing at the concert, she's going away.
    POINT

    ....

5   Don't you remember anything about your life in India as a child?
    RECOLLECTION

    ....

6   Someone had told him that honey could be used as an antiseptic.
    HEARD

    ....

7   My car costs me about £200 a year to run.
    SPEND

    ....

8   His statement to the Police was inconsistent with the report he made to the
    Insurance Company.
    AGREE

    ....

9   I lent Caroline ten pounds to buy that dress.
    OWES

    ....

10 He had no thought of going to America.
    NOTHING

    ....

SECTION B

5. Read the following passage, and then answer the questions which follow it.

   And so you ask me to tell you how I manage to endure this monotonous
country life; how, fond as I am of excitement, adventure, society, art, I go cheer-
fully through the daily routine of a commonplace country profession, never
requiring a six-weeks' holiday; not caring to see Europe, hardly ever spending
5 a day in London; having never actually got to Paris.
   You wonder why I do not grow as dull as those round me, whose talk is of
farming – as indeed mine is, often enough; why I have not been tempted to bury
myself in my study, and live a life of dreams among old books.
   I will tell you. I am a minute philosopher. I am possibly, after all, a man of
10 small mind, content with small pleasures. Meanwhile I can understand your

surprise, though you cannot understand my content; for before I was twenty-three, I discovered that my lot was to stay at home and earn my bread in a quiet way; that England from now on, was to be my prison or my palace, as I should choose to make it; and I have made it the latter.

15 I will confess to you, though, that in those first years of my youth, this little England – or rather, this little patch of moorland in which I have struck roots – looked at moments more like a prison than a palace; then my foolish young heart would sigh, "Oh! that I had wings" to swoop over land and sea in a self-glorifying fashion. But the thirst for adventure and excitement was strong in
20 me, as perhaps it ought to be in all at twenty-one. Others went out to see the glorious new worlds of the West, the glorious old worlds of the East – why shouldn't I? But when one finds one's self on the wrong side of forty, and the first grey hairs begin to show on the temples, why, then one makes a virtue of necessity; and if one still longs for sights one takes the nearest, and looks for
25 wonders, not in distant mountains, but in the lawn in the garden.

For there it is, the whole infinite miracle of nature in every blade of grass, if we only have eyes to see it; and in that moorland which I call my winter-garden I contrive to find as much health and amusement as I have time for – and who ought to have more? I call the garden mine, not because I own it in any legal
30 sense, but because ten thousand people can own the same thing if they view its beauty with pleasure.

Besides, my delight in my garden is a cheap one. It costs me not one penny in upkeep. And is it not true wealth to have all I want without paying for it? To have the whole universe; the sun and frost, wind and rain, planting and colour-
35 ing my winter-garden for me, without my having to do anything except admire it?

Yes, I am very rich. In the doings of our little country neighbourhood I find tragedy and comedy, too fantastic, sometimes too sad, to be written down. In the fifteen miles of moorland I find the materials of all possible physical science.
40 How can I be richer, if I have lying at my feet all day, a thousand times more wealth than I can use?

Some people would complain of such a life, in such a "narrow sphere," and call it monotonous. Very likely it is so. But is monotony in itself an evil? Which is better, to know many places slightly, or to know one place well? I learn more
45 studying over and over again the same familiar sights, than I should roaming all over Europe in search of new wonders.

As for doing fine things, I have learnt to believe that I am not set to do them, simply because I am not able to do them; and as for seeing fine things, I have learnt to see the sight which lies nearest me. In any life there will always be
50 sufficient to occupy a minute philosopher.

1 The author explains that he is able to bear life in the country because

....

2 How does the author's present opinion about England differ from when

he was young? ....

....

3 Why is the author's "winter-garden" important to him? ....

....

4   The author doesn't have to pay anything for the upkeep of the garden because ....

5   Why is monotony not considered an evil in the passage? ....
....

6   "as indeed mine is" (l. 7) refers to ....
....

7   To what does the phrase "earn my bread" (l. 12) usually refer? ....
....

8   What does "struck roots" (l. 16) mean? ....
....

9   What is the meaning of "makes a virtue of necessity"? (ll. 23–24)
....

10 The author considers the garden his because ....
....

11 What does the author mean by "In the doings"? (l. 37) ....
....

12 Why does the author say he has "more wealth than I can use"? (ll. 40–41)
....

13 What is meant by a "narrow sphere"? (l. 42) ....
....

14 Which best explains the use of "roaming"? (l. 45) walking / wandering / straying / marching ....

15 "to know many places slightly" (l. 44) means? ....
....

16 Does the author think himself capable of doing fine things? If not, why not?
....
....

17 What do you think the author means by "a minute philosopher"? (l. 50)

....

....

18 In a paragraph of not more than 100 words show how the author is able
to find contentment in country life. ....

....

....

....

....

....

....

....

....

....

....

SECTION C

6. Your local children's hospital, which has served the community well for
over fifty years, is to be closed, and amalgamated with the County Hospital
twenty miles away. A meeting of local residents to protest against this decision
is to be held next month, and will also be attended by representatives from the
County Hospital.

As a resident of twenty years' standing and the parent of four young children
you have been asked to make the opening speech. Begin as follows and go on
to complete your speech: write another 125–175 words.

"Ladies and Gentlemen, I don't need to tell you with what dismay we first
learned of the decision to close St Theresa's Hospital ....

PAPER 4: LISTENING COMPREHENSION (40 minutes)

The passages on which these questions are based will be found in the Appendix.

First Passage

1 On the part of the beach where Joanna was standing the sand was
   A   untrodden and perfectly smooth
   B   ruffled and ridged with silver
   C   formed into ridges by projecting rocks
   D   unlittered and patterned by the wind

2 From the description given in the passage, what was the general shape of Abbot's Island?
   A   rectangular
   B   curved
   C   semi-circular
   D   pointed

3 Why do you think the writer uses the word "treacherous" in connection with the island?
   A   only a small boat could navigate its way through the rocks
   B   the surrounding waters had to be navigated with care
   C   the island formed a sandbank across the bay
   D   it was impossible to land on it

4 When Joanna first saw the man on the island, she thought
   A   he must have just flown on to the island
   B   he was trying to fly off the island
   C   he wanted to identify himself
   D   he wanted to attract attention

5 What was it that made Joanna suddenly remember the story of the drowned Abbot?
   A   The suspicious movements of the man's arms
   B   The ceremonial manner of the man's movements
   C   The meaning conveyed by the man's dancing
   D   The ghostlike appearance of the man

Second Passage

6 From this advertisement, it would seem that the Company is only interested in recruiting girls who
   A   have already taken a secretarial course at school
   B   want to become fully trained secretaries
   C   are interested in a job with good prospects
   D   have had previous secretarial experience

7 Girls accepted for part-time typing training courses

A work as junior clerks in the Training Department
B spend two hours a day in the Typing Service
C attend a full-time course after five weeks
D attend a full-time course after several months

8 Girls of 16–17 may be selected for full-time typing courses provided that they

A have had three months' experience as typists
B take an examination at the end of three months
C can show evidence of having reached a good educational standard
D expect to achieve good grades in their examinations

9 Candidates for the full-time secretarial courses

A will be expected to take two subjects at "A" level during their training
B will already be proficient in shorthand and typing
C will have reached "A" level standard at school
D will be expected to be fully-trained at the end of three months

10 As far as promotion is concerned, the Company makes it clear that this will depend on

A a yearly assessment of ability
B an assessment of skills
C practical training
D length of training

Third Passage

11 From this account we understand that the two British climbers

A had been unable to reach the summit of Mount Everest by a direct route
B had climbed to a height of 29,028 feet
C had reached the south-east face of the mountain with difficulty
D had been the first people to climb to the summit of Mount Everest

12 It would seem that the leader of the expedition had

A expected to reach the summit before the rest of his party
B calculated how long it would take to reach the summit
C planned to reach the summit in five weeks
D expected to climb the mountain in record time

13 From the information given in the passage we learn that

A it takes three weeks to climb Mount Everest
B the Himalayan winter lasts three weeks
C good weather is not expected for at least another three weeks
D another three weeks of good weather is expected

14 The camp from which the two climbers made their final successful attempt was
    A on a steep rock projecting from the face of the mountain
    B on a cliff 26,500 feet up the mountain
    C blocked by a rock dislodged by previous climbers
    D higher than 26,500 feet up the mountain

15 Why was the route taken by the two climbers considered to be a dangerous challenge?
    A It was necessary to traverse a treacherous snowfield
    B The thin air made it impossible to breathe
    C The atmosphere presented serious hazards
    D It was connected to the south-east col by a gulley

Fourth Passage

16 Why was it difficult to reach the Police Station at Brightstone Beach?
    A it was practically inaccessible
    B it was built at an angle
    C it was completely isolated
    D it was practically invisible

17 What impression do we receive of Sergeant Beckett?
    A he was primarily a seafaring man
    B he contrived to go fishing most afternoons
    C he was not anxious for advancement
    D he liked interfering in other people's business

18 How did Charles eventually reach the part of the beach where Beckett was seated?
    A by climbing over some sharp rocks
    B by scrambling up some steep steps
    C by edging himself down a rock
    D by slithering down some steps

19 Looking at the cliffs, it was possible to measure the passage of time by
    A the enormous size of the rocks
    B the formation of the rocks
    C the changing colour of the rocks
    D the solidity of the rocks

20 How was Charles affected when he looked up at the cliffs?
    A he felt awed by them
    B he thought they seemed very mysterious
    C he felt very old
    D he thought they seemed insignificant

PAPER 5: INTERVIEW (12 minutes)

Section A *Photograph*

Look at this photograph carefully and be prepared to answer some questions about it.

Describe the scene in the photograph.
What do you think this machine is used for?
Why do you think it is situated in the country away from buildings?
Would you consider it pleasant or unpleasant to work with such machines?

Importance of radio telecommunication.
Candidate's interest in scientific work.
Possibility of signals being received from unknown sources in outer space.
Increasing interest in the detection of new stars in space.

Section B *Topics*

Choose one of the following topics and prepare to give your views on it, for 1½ to 2 minutes. You may make notes, but do not try to write out a whole speech.

1   How far does success depend on personal appearance?

2   The causes of cruelty to children

3   Is it desirable for young people to live away from their families?

Section C *Dialogue*

(Prepare yourself to read the part of the STUDENT. Your teacher will read the other part.)

STUDENT: Oh, hello. I've just been listening to another of those programmes on the decadence of modern youth. You'd think some of these people on radio had come into the world as octogenarians. Just because we have long hair and wear T-shirts and jeans, we're branded as hooligans or drop-outs. As a matter of fact I'm one of the most law-abiding people I know. Take my father, for instance –

Friend: Just a minute –

STUDENT: Don't interrupt. That's the trouble with you, you're always interrupting just when I'm getting into my stride. Now, what was I saying? Oh yes, my parents – look at my father, always fiddling his Income Tax returns and having expense account lunches with some ghastly client or other. Petty dishonesty and hypocrisy, that's all it is, and as for my mother –

Friend: Do listen a moment –

STUDENT: And mother – always running round with that pseudo-intellectual circle of hers – coffee parties and jumble sales and poetry readings – all in the name of charity. It's nothing but a snob racket, to say nothing of being a smokescreen to hide the fact that she hasn't got anything better to do with her time –

Friend: Look, I'm trying to tell you –

STUDENT: And I'm trying to tell you. It's jealousy, that's all it is. All this criticism and carping about the youth of today, and how the old practised self-denial in the last war, and respected their elders, and were grateful for the miserable opportunities that came their way. All I can say is, they must have been as boring and self-satisfied then as they are now –

Friend: For the last time, will you listen? There's a man at the door – says it's urgent.

STUDENT: Why on earth didn't you say so?

Friend: You didn't give me a chance.

STUDENT: Urgent? It's probably only someone trying to con me into buying an encyclopaedia.

Friend: It's a man from the Gas Company. Seems you haven't paid your bill and he's threatening to cut you off. Probably done it too, while you've been talking.

Section D *Situations*

1 While on holiday you spend the night at a small hotel, but when you receive your bill you find that you have been overcharged. Ask for an explanation.

2 The Staff Canteen where you work is expensive and badly run. As a senior member of the staff, you have been asked to complain to the Manager. Give reasons.

3 A friend, whom you offered to put up for two nights in your small flat, has now been with you for over a month and shows no sign of going. Ask him/her politely to leave.

4 You have to meet a friend who is arriving at London Airport next Saturday, but you do not know the Flight number or time of arrival. Telephone the Airport and make enquiries.

5 You come out of the cinema to find that your car, which you left in the car park, has been stolen. Go to the Police Station and report the loss.

TEST FOUR

PAPER 1: COMPOSITION (3 hours)

Answer questions 1, 2 and 3. You should spend about the same amount of time on each.

Section A

1. **Either** (*a*) The Year 2000. What sociological changes would you expect to have taken place?

   or (*b*) The seashore – the effect of its constantly changing scene on Man.

2. **Either** (*a*) "Behaviour is conditioned by environment." Discuss.

   or (*b*) "Man is a naturally aggressive animal." How far, in your opinion, is this a true statement?

Section B

3. Read the following passage and then answer the questions which follow it.

   I have sometimes thought that the enjoyment of the Classics is marred by the manner in which they are presented to us. We are seldom, for instance, allowed to "discover" Shakespeare. We are introduced to his plays in the schoolroom, usually at an age when our knowledge of life is too limited for us to be able to
5 make head or tail of the great speeches. Nor, if we are attracted by the magic of the words, are we allowed to absorb them, to curl our tongues round them, without interruption. We are subjected to a daunting experience known as "English Lit." in which, at a set hour every week, a work of genius is offered up for interpretation and dissection by lesser minds, processed in fact in preparation for
10 "Examinations", by which time the magic will have gone out of it for most of us, and those with the best memories will get the best marks. Does it, I wonder, ever occur to those studious heads bent over their books, or the less studious stifling their yawns, that the vast majority of great literature was written to be enjoyed by ordinary people with no thought of examinations, and that on the
15 success or otherwise of such works depended the livelihood of the writer – not excluding Shakespeare.
   How exciting it would be to attend a performance of *Hamlet* or *Romeo and Juliet* for the first time without having been painstakingly prepared beforehand. To receive one's own unadulterated impression, to applaud or condemn with as
20 open a mind as the playgoers of Shakespeare's age. How rewarding to read a great novel for no better reason than the fun of wanting to know what was going to happen next.

I remember, as a child, coming across a volume of poetry and, fascinated by
its rhythms, taking it to bed with me to read aloud. I did not understand half of
25 it, but the words made music when repeated and conjured up pictures as colour-
ful and fascinating as the fairy tales which up till then had fired my imagination.
The poems were by John Donne, I believe, a poet usually considered unsuitable
for youthful reading. Whatever they were, they awakened in me a sense of the
beauty of words and a lifelong love of reading for its own sake.

(*a*) What does the writer mean by the phrase "to 'discover' Shakespeare"? (l. 3)

(*b*) Comment on the writer's choice of the word "absorb". (l. 6)

(*c*) Explain what the writer means by describing our introduction to English
Literature as a "daunting experience". (l. 7)

(*d*) What image is evoked by the word "processed" (l. 9) and to what does
it refer?

(*e*) ". . . the magic will have gone out of it." (l. 10)
What is the significance of this sentence in relation to the theme?

(*f*) Comment on the writer's use of the word "unadulterated". (l. 19)

(*g*) What impression do you receive from the expression "conjured up" (l. 25)
in the writer's account of reading poetry as a child?

PAPER 2: READING COMPREHENSION (1¼ hours)

Section A

Choose the word or phrase which best completes each sentence. **Give one
answer only** to each question.

1 The recent confusion over rateable values is an _____ example of the
Council's inefficiency.
A outward   B outgoing   C outstanding   D outspoken
E outgrown

2 The guard fired and missed the escaping prisoner by _____ .
A a heartbeat   B a hair's breadth   C a short head
D a long nose   E a long shot

3 We are raising money for handicapped children, would you care to
put _____ in the collecting box?
A a donation   B a bequest   C a credit   D an advance
E an allowance

4 Mr Hopkins, who lost a leg in a car accident, has now been fitted with
_____ limb.
A a substitute   B an artificial   C a superficial   D an attached
E an extra

5   To their dismay, the children on the beach found that they had been _____ by the tide.
    A   turned off   B   put off   C   cut off   D   taken off   E   shut off

6   When I took his temperature, it was two degrees above _____.
    A   average   B   ordinary   C   regular   D   normal   E   usual

7   My brother has just had central heating _____ in his flat.
    A   inducted   B   introduced   C   inlaid   D   inset   E   installed

8   I don't think the charge for redecorating the house is excessive in _____ to its size.
    A   correspondence   B   equation   C   proportion   D   dimension
    E   measurement

9   We didn't plan to stay in the same hotel as the Browns, it was just a _____.
    A   happening   B   coincidence   C   occurrence   D   casualty
    E   chance

10 Mrs Simpson will never be able _____ the damp winter in England because of her health.
    A   to repel   B   to repulse   C   to stand   D   to sustain
    E   to resist

11 When Andrew opened his violin case, he found that someone had stolen his _____.
    A   stick   B   rod   C   arc   D   bow   E   oar

12 In spite of the terrible storm, the ship was _____.
    A   uninjured   B   unbroken   C   uncut   D   unhurt
    E   undamaged

13 The electricity failure is not dangerous. There is no need for _____.
    A   cowardice   B   alarm   C   scare   D   dread   E   stage-fright

14 If you don't complete your income tax _____, you may have to pay more tax than is necessary.
    A   report   B   receipt   C   document   D   return   E   account

15 The illness from which Alice is suffering has now been _____ as pneumonia.
    A   diagnosed   B   determined   C   discovered   D   deduced
    E   detailed

16 My father is a very wise man, but even so, I don't think his judgments are always _____.
    A   unmistakable   B   infallible   C   certifiable   D   veritable
    E   actual

17 A new _____ of Winston Churchill will be published in November.
    A   history   B   autobiography   C   narrative   D   biography
    E   book

18 I am going to have this snapshot of Michael and Angela _____.
    A   amplified   B   inflated   C   extended   D   expanded
    E   enlarged

19 There is a memorial _____ in the church commemorating the soldiers who fell in the last war.
    A   grave   B   block   C   stone   D   tile   E   strip

20 I feel that Mr Anderson's efforts to help the poor in this neighbourhood have not been sufficiently _____ .
    A estimated   B calculated   C advocated   D exalted
    E appreciated

21 I am allergic to mussels. If I eat them I always come out in a _____ .
    A bruise   B swelling   C rash   D mange   E pimple

22 The Railway Union has agreed to allow its claim to be settled by _____ .
    A mediation   B dissentation   C arbitration   D adjudication
    E judgment

23 When the police burst into the room, the injured woman was lying _____ on the bed.
    A full-length   B elongated   C strung-out   D long-drawn-out
    E at length

24 If you want this apple tree to bear good fruit next year, you will have _____ it.
    A to pare   B to nip   C to whittle   D to prune   E to taper

25 The ancient sailing ships usually had a _____ of a woman on the prow.
    A face-lift   B figurehead   C feature   D frontispiece
    E frontage

26 Do straighten that picture over the piano, it looks _____ from here.
    A bent   B inclined   C crooked   D uneven   E indirect

27 When the ship docked at Southampton, they found a _____ in the hold.
    A stowaway   B trespasser   C interloper   D squatter
    E gate-crasher

28 If you don't want your bicycle to be stolen, you should put _____ on it.
    A a handcuff   B a fetter   C a latch   D a screw
    E a padlock

29 If you paint the walls cream, I think it will _____ the colour of the curtains better.
    A take out   B throw out   C lift out   D bring out
    E make out

30 The witness _____ the statements made by the accused man.
    A corroborated   B testified   C deposed   D agreed
    E confessed

31 I think the pattern of that wallpaper has been printed _____ .
    A back to back   B face down   C upside down
    D round and round   E side to side

32 All the windows of the house were _____ by the explosion.
    A crashed   B crushed   C shattered   D shredded
    E crumbled

33 I have been advised to take every _____ against catching 'flu again this winter.
    A prevention   B precaution   C premeditation   D prediction
    E predilection

34 After considering the evidence for three hours, the Jury came to _____ verdict.
    A   a unanimous   B   a united   C   an undivided
    D   an unambiguous   E   an unadulterated

35 The Manager has _____ to dismiss Hopkins, if he continues to come late every morning.
    A   menaced   B   warned   C   alerted   D   threatened
    E   foretold

36 Annabelle looks _____ of her former self since her long illness.
    A   an illusion   B   an image   C   a shade   D   a phantom
    E   a shadow

37 Leave the shirt _____ in cold water overnight and the stains will soon come out.
    A   to drench   B   to drip   C   to soak   D   to marinate
    E   to float

38 The Chancellor of the Exchequer warned the nation that they would all have to _____ if they wanted to overcome the present economic crisis.
    A   tip the scale   B   tighten their belts   C   come to heel
    D   close their ranks   E   bite the dust

39 If you buy Unity Bonds, you will get a good return on your _____.
    A   wealth   B   balance   C   exchange   D   capital   E   currency

40 I can't afford to buy that colour television set, the cost is _____.
    A   prohibited   B   prohibitive   C   proscribed   D   prodigal
    E   provocative

Section B

In this section you will find after each of the passages a number of questions or unfinished statements about the passage, each with four suggested ways of finishing it. You must choose the one which you think fits best. **Give one answer only** to each question.

First Passage

I hope I did not look as yellow as I felt when I stood to take the plunge; I have never been so sick with fear before or since. "Remember, one hand for your eyes," said someone from a thousand miles off, and I dived.

I do not suppose it is really true that the eyes of an octopus shine in the dark;
5 besides, it was clear daylight only six feet down in the limpid water; but I could have sworn the brute's eyes burned at me as I turned in towards his cranny. That dark glow, whatever may have been its origin, was the last thing I saw as I blacked out with my left hand and rose into his clutches. Then, I remember chiefly a dreadful sliminess with a herculean power behind it. Something whipped
10 round my left forearm and the back of my neck, binding the two together. In the same flash, another something slapped itself high on my forehead, and I felt it crawling down inside the back of my vest. My impulse was to tear at it with my right hand, but I felt the whole of that arm pinioned to my ribs. In most emergencies the mind works with crystal-clear impersonality. This was not even
15 an emergency, for I knew myself perfectly safe as my companion was near. But

my boyhood's nightmare was upon me, when I felt the swift constriction of those disgusting arms jerk my head and shoulders in towards the reef, and my mind went blank of every thought save the beastliness of contact with that squat head. A mouth began to muzzle below my throat, at the junction of the collar-bones.
20 I forgot there was anyone to save me. Yet something still directed me to hold my breath.

I was awakened from my cowardly trance by a quick strong pull on my shoulders, back from the cranny. The tentacles around me tightened painfully, but I knew I was adrift from the reef. I gave a kick, rose to the surface and turned
25 on my back with the brute sticking out of my chest like a tumour. My mouth was smothered by some flabby moving horror. The suckers felt like hot rings pulling at my skin. It was only seconds, I suppose, from then to the attack of my deliverer, but it seemed like a century of nausea.

My friend came up between me and the reef. He pounced, pulled, bit down,
30 and the thing was over – for everyone but me. At that sudden relaxation of the tentacles, I let out a great breath, sank, and drew in the next under water. It took the combined help of both boys to get me, coughing, heaving and pretending to join in their delighted laughter, back to the reef. I had to submit there to a kind of war-dance round me, in which the dead beast was slung whizzing past
35 my head from one to the other. I had a chance to observe then that it was not by any stretch of fancy a giant, but just plain average. That took the bulge out of my budding self-esteem. I left hurriedly for the cover of the jetty, and was sick.

41 Why was it difficult for the author to hear what someone said before he dived?

   A he was too far away
   B he was already in the water
   C he was vomiting with fright
   D he was stricken with fright

42 The author was able to see the eyes of the octopus only briefly as he

   A soon became unconscious
   B concealed his own eyes
   C covered the eyes of the octopus
   D couldn't see well in the dark water

43 From the passage we understand that an octopus will attack by

   A trying to drown its victim
   B trying to crush its victims
   C sucking its victims into a cranny
   D tearing its victims apart

44 "with crystal-clear impersonality" means

   A objectively
   B subjectively
   C unfeelingly
   D impartially

45 The nausea felt by the author stemmed from

A his experiences as a boy
B the irrational terrors of boyhood
C the long-forgotten dreams of boyhood
D his day dreams as a boy

46 The author didn't breathe out under water as

A there was no one to save him
B he remembered someone would save him
C he remembered some old instructions
D he reacted instinctively

47 What helped the author avoid being pulled into the cranny?

A kicking hard and reaching the surface
B being dragged back from behind
C being woken up suddenly
D floating away from the reef

48 When he reached the surface the author

A called for help
B was rescued immediately
C lost track of time
D found his skin was burnt

49 The author started to cough and splutter under water because

A he let his breath out
B he stopped breathing
C he inhaled suddenly
D he held his breath

50 We understand that the author was rather proud of himself until

A he saw the octopus clearly
B his friends made him dance
C he was violently sick
D his friends threw the octopus about

Second Passage

Anyone who thinks exploration always involves long journeys should have his head examined. Or, better, he should put on his oldest clothes and go off in search of a junk shop. There are three kinds – one full of discarded books, one full of discarded Government equipment, and one full of discarded anything.
5 A junk shop may have four walls and a roof, or it may be no more than a trestle-table in an open air market; but there is one infallible test: no genuine junk shopkeeper will ever pester you to make up your mind and buy something. And you are no true junk shopper if you march purposefully round the shop as if you knew exactly what you wanted. You must browse, gently chewing the cud of
10 your idle thoughts, and nibbling here and there at a sight or a touch of the goods that lie about you. Yet you must also possess a penetrating glance, darting your eyes about you to spot the treasures that may lurk beneath the rubbish. This is

what makes junk shopping such a satisfying voyage of exploration. You never know what interesting and unexpected thing you may discover next. For in a
15 true junk shop, not even the proprietor is always quite sure what his dusty stock conceals. There is always the chance that you may pick up a first edition, a pair of exotic ear-rings, a piece of early Wedgwood china, or a cine camera – and possess it for the price of fifty cigarettes.

But this kind of treasure hunt is only a sideline to the true junk shopper. The
20 real attraction lies in finding something that catches your own especial fancy, though everybody else may pass it by. An ancient tarnished clock, whose brass beneath your hands will shine anew; empty boxes that you can see transformed into the framework of a bookcase; an old bound volume of magazines of three-quarters of a century ago, which will shed strange sidelights on the ways our
25 great-grandparents behaved and looked at life.

When you begin junk shopping, half the attraction is that you go with absolutely no intention of buying anything. You spend your first couple of Saturday afternoons ambling around among dusty shelves, savouring a page or a chapter as you please, or fingering the piles of oddments that litter counters or tables.
30 At first, be warned, don't try to buy. You may, indeed you should, ask the price of this and that; but just to give you an idea of what the junk shopkeeper thinks you might be willing to pay him.

Later, you will find yourself returning a second and third time to something which has caught your fancy. And when you can hold back no longer, bargaining
35 begins in earnest. This is the other great attraction of the true junk shop. Not only may it hold every conceivable product from every imaginable country; it also transports you to the mediaeval market place or the oriental bazaar, where no price is fixed until buyer and seller have waged a friendly war together, and proved each other's mettle. And this is where your old clothes become impor-
40 tant: let no one take you for a rich connoisseur, or you will find yourself paying a rich man's prices. And avoid at all costs the suspicion of an American accent, or in spite of the good nature of all good junk shopkeepers, you will be for it.

51   The author equates junk hunting with exploration because both involve

    A   travelling long distances
    B   careful preparation
    C   a spirit of adventure
    D   discovering unheard of places

52   We understand from the passage that a genuine junk shop is a place

    A   full of worthless things
    B   where no one bothers you
    C   which sells only rubbish
    D   where no one wants to buy

53   "gently chewing the cud of your idle thoughts" implies that the junk hunter is

    A   eating sweets or gum as he wanders around
    B   not thinking of anything
    C   ruminating on this and that
    D   thinking of many things at the same time

54   What quality does the author consider a good junk hunter should possess?

    A   perfect eyesight
    B   alertness
    C   casualness
    D   impatience

55   According to the passage a true junk hunter hopes to

    A   find a bargain
    B   discover something new
    C   discover something exotic
    D   find something invaluable

56   By asking the price of an object, the junk hunter gets a good idea of

    A   its value
    B   the shopkeeper's evaluation
    C   how much to offer
    D   its age

57   The author suggests that the junk buyer's main reason for bargaining is

    A   to fix a price
    B   because he hasn't enough money
    C   because it's expected
    D   to ask a price

58   Why does a junk shop remind the author of a market or bazaar?

    A   they sell the same kind of goods
    B   their method of selling is the same
    C   the customers always quarrel before buying
    D   their location is similar

59   "proved each other's mettle" means

    A   agreed a certain price
    B   argued amicably
    C   tested one another
    D   showed their trust

60   From the passage we understand that speaking   ith an American accent

    A   arouses suspicion in the junk shopkeeper
    B   increases the price of the goods
    C   engenders friendliness in the shopkeeper
    D   increases the chance of bargaining

PAPER 3: USE OF ENGLISH (3 hours)

SECTION A

1. Fill each of the numbered blanks in the passage with **one** suitable word.

I wonder how _____(1) it is still _____(2) to say that crime doesn't _____(3). One has only to open the newspapers to be _____(4) with some report of hijacking, kidnapping or the taking of _____(5), actions undertaken in the hope of forcing authority to _____(6) to some outrageous _____(7). A study of these methods seems to _____(8) that they are outstandingly successful, and that so _____(9) as the criminal keeps a cool _____(10) and a gun in his hand, he remains in _____(11) of the situation and usually gets what he wants, because _____(12) Government wishes to be held _____(13) for the _____(14) of innocent lives. There does not appear to be any reliable _____(15) for criminal acts of this kind, which are frequently carried _____(16) in the name of political or religious ideals. Each case _____(17) its own _____(18) and although much experience has been _____(19), no satisfactory solution has yet been found and society continues to be held to _____(20) by a vicious minority.

2. Finish each of the following sentences in such a way that it means the same as the sentence printed before it.

Example: Are these two rooms the same size?

Answer: Is there any difference *in the size of these two rooms*?

Louise tried to comfort the little boy as best she could.

1 Louise did..

Would it interest you to come to Art classes next term?

2 <u>Would you be</u>...?

I can't believe John refused to insure Mary's ring.

3 <u>Surely John</u>...

They found the Prime Minister's broadcast impressive.

4 <u>They were</u>...

Why is Sarah always so tired in the mornings?

5 <u>Is there</u> ....?

If you happen to see him, ask him to telephone me tonight.

6 <u>Should</u>...

Mary believes nothing her husband tells her.

7 <u>Whatever</u> ....

The flight from London to Dublin was exactly an hour.

8 <u>It took</u>...

I'm sure it was the man in dark glasses who murdered his wife.

9 <u>It must</u>...

Whose is that brief case on the table?

10 <u>Who does</u> ....?

3. Fill each of the numbered blanks with a suitable word or phrase.

Example: If the house caught fire, what ....?

Answer: If the house caught fire, what *would you do*?

1 Although it was only five miles to the station, we ....
   .... there.

2 Shall I telephone Mr Stephenson now?
   No, he .... from lunch yet.

3   I can't open this tin of soup, because .... the tin-opener is.

4   Ever since I was a child, I .... the Taj Mahal.

5   "Hurry up, Susan, your father's waiting for you downstairs!"

   "All right, ... in a minute."

6   Alice .... her degree, she's too lazy.

7   "Go and tell the children lunch is ready, please, Mary."

   "I .... them. They're washing their hands now."

8   If only ...., I'd have met you at the airport myself.

9   "Laurence says he's never going to speak to me again!"

   "Oh, don't take any notice of him, he's .... that."

10 "I was late for work again this morning."

   "I can't think .... a bit earlier."

4. For each of the sentences below, write a new sentence **as similar as possible in meaning to the original sentence,** but using the word given in capital letters.

Example: Your hair is much too long.
       NEEDS

Answer: *Your hair needs cutting.*

1   Do you think he always tells the truth?
   LIES

   ....

2   No-one could hear what the lecturer said.
   INAUDIBLE

   ....

3   I was able to make good use of this Italian Phrase Book in Rome.
   HANDY

   ....

4   We never mention my father's disability at home.
    SPOKEN

    ....

5   The Manager has asked me to consider this proposal very carefully.
    CONSIDERATION

    ....

6   In my opinion, Income Tax will be raised in the next Budget.
    ASK

    ....

7   There is no way out of this dilemma.
    IMPOSSIBLE

    ....

8   Are you quite sure you can only come on Saturday?
    IS

    ....

9   It's quite unnecessary to hoover the sitting-room, I did it this morning.
    NECESSITY

    ....

10 That's the last time I ask the Welfare Officer for help.
    NEVER

    ....

SECTION B

5. Read the following passage, and then answer the questions which follow it.

We are moving inexorably into the age of automation. Our aim is not to devise a mechanism which can perform a thousand different actions of any individual man but, on the contrary, one which could by a single action replace a thousand men.
5   Industrial automation has moved along three lines. First there is the conveyor belt system of continuous production whereby separate operations are linked into a single sequence. The goods produced by this well-established method are untouched by the worker, and the machine replaces both unskilled and semi-skilled. Secondly, there is automation with feedback control of the quality of
10 the product; here mechanisms are built into the system which can compare the output with a norm, that is, the actual product with what it is supposed to be, and then correct any shortcomings. The entire cycle of operations dispenses with human control except in so far as monitors are concerned. One or two

examples of this type of automation will illustrate its immense possibilities.
15 There is a factory in the U.S.A. which makes 1,000 million electric light bulbs a year, and the factory employs three hundred people. If the preautomation techniques were to be employed, the labour force required would leap to 25,000. A motor manufacturing company with 45,000 spare parts regulates their entire supply entirely by computer. Computers can be entrusted with most of the
20 supervision of industrial installations, such as chemical plants or oil refineries. Thirdly, there is computer automation, for banks, accounting departments, insurance companies and the like. Here the essential features are the recording, storing, sorting and retrieval of information.

The principal merit of modern computing machines is the achievement of
25 their vastly greater speed of operation by comparison with unaided human effort; a task which otherwise might take years, if attempted at all, now takes days or hours.

One of the most urgent problems of industrial societies rapidly introducing automation is how to fill the time that will be made free by the machines which
30 will take over the tasks of the workers. The question is not simply of filling empty time but also of utilizing the surplus human energy that will be released. We are already seeing straws in the wind: destructive outbursts on the part of youth whose work no longer demands muscular strength. While automation will undoubtedly do away with a large number of tedious jobs, are we sure that it will
35 not put others which are equally tedious in their place? For an enormous amount of sheer monitoring will be required. A man in an automated plant may have to sit for hours on end watching dials and taking decisive action when some signal informs him that all is not well. What meaning will his occupation bear for the worker? How will he devote his free time after a four or five hour stint of labour?
40 Moreover, what, indeed, will be the significance for him of his leisure? If industry of the future could be purged of its monotony and meaninglessness, man would then be better equipped to use his leisure time constructively.

1 The main purpose of automation is ....

....

2 Why are less men required for the first type of industrial automation than in a manual system? ....

....

3 What is more sophisticated about the second industrial automation system than the first? ....

....

4 What is the chief benefit of computing machines? ....

....

5 One of the biggest drawbacks of automation in industrial societies is ......

....

6 How would the sense be changed if the phrase "a single action" (l. 3) were replaced by "a thousand actions"? ....

....

7 What is the meaning of the phrase "a single sequence"? (l. 7).................

....

8 What is the comparison of "the output with a norm" (l. 11) to which the author refers? ....

....

9 "their" (in l. 18) refers to ....

10 What are the "essential features"? (l.22) ....

....

11 The phrase "if attempted at all" (l. 26) refers to ....

12 What connection is there between the words "urgent" and "rapidly"? (l. 28)

....

13 What does the author consider as important as "filling empty time"? (ll. 30–31) ....

14 What is meant by the phrase "straws in the wind"? (l. 32) ....

....

15 "Sheer monitoring" (l. 36) means ....

16 Which of the following best explains the use of "stint"? (l. 39) effort/force/ excess/stretch/term ....

17 What are the three lines of industrial automation referred to by the author?

....

....

....

18 In a paragraph of not more than 100 words, describe the benefits and problems of increasing industrial automation.

....

....

....

....

....

....

....

....

....

....

SECTION C

GALLOWS CROSSING
SECOND CHILD KILLED
MOTHERS IN UPROAR

6. These headlines appeared in a national newspaper above a report of the death of a child in a car accident at a dangerous crossing where the installation of traffic lights has been delayed owing to economy cuts in the local Council's budget. Write a letter to your M.P. enlisting his aid in getting traffic lights installed. Begin your letter as follows, and write another 125–175 words:

James Preston, M.P.
HOUSE OF COMMONS
London S.W.1.

Sir,
   I am writing to draw your urgent attention to ....

PAPER 4: LISTENING COMPREHENSION (40 minutes)

The passages on which these questions are based will be found in the Appendix.

First Passage

1 Torbay Hall came on to the market because
   A It had been the home of a famous artist
   B the previous owner had died there
   C the previous owner had no heirs
   D it was no longer needed as a family residence

2 We understand that Torbay Hall is deservedly well-known for
   A the peach trees growing in the garden
   B the fine fruit from its orchard
   C the design of its hothouse
   D the quality of some of its fruit

3 It is often difficult for physically handicapped people to enjoy staying in hotels because
   A they feel they are unwelcome
   B they are afraid of making trouble
   C they encounter too many difficulties
   D they make too many difficulties

4 The bulk of the money required for the project has come from
   A individual donations
   B Government funds
   C an American charity
   D physically-handicapped Americans

5 From the passage it would seem that Torbay Hall will not be able to offer separate accommodation to
   A more than forty families at a time
   B more than two large families at a time
   C single people without families
   D single people in shared flats

Second Passage

6 When compared with good characters, bad characters in fiction
   A excite our compassion more easily
   B involve our feelings more deeply
   C condition us to accept more suffering
   D arouse our worst feelings more strongly

7   According to the writer, the function of the bad character in fiction is to

A   prevent us from becoming insipid
B   prevent us from becoming boring
C   make the other characters seem more exciting
D   capture our interest more readily

8   It would seem that what we admire most about our fictional heroes is

A   the successful outcome of their actions
B   the essential goodness of their actions
C   their caution in the face of danger
D   their secretiveness in the face of danger

9   The writer comes to the conclusion that ordinary people

A   would like to go back to a less authoritarian existence
B   would be ill at ease in a less authoritarian existence
C   haven't sufficient courage to defy authority
D   are content to blame the Government for their dull lives

10   According to the established conventions of fiction

A   the wicked usually come to a bad end
B   the good only die at the end
C   the wicked usually die in the end
D   the good cannot survive to the end

Third Passage

11   The difficulties of Ferguson's climb to the top of St Peter's Mount were aggravated by

A   the sheep grazing on the track
B   the heaviness of the wet bracken
C   the slipperiness of the scrub
D   the ill-defined course of the track

12   Ferguson decided to continue his climb in spite of the mist on the summit because

A   he had gone too far to turn back
B   he had not gone far enough to turn back
C   he had already reached halfway
D   he had yet to reach halfway

13   What happened to Ferguson when the mist drifted down round him?

A   he went blind
B   he lost his glasses
C   his vision was affected
D   he saw a vision

14   Why do you think Ferguson was so exhausted when he finally reached the top?

    A   he was too old for hill-climbing
    B   he had no experience of hill-climbing
    C   he was not in training for hill-climbing
    D   he was physically too ill for hill-climbing

15   The writer describes the view from the summit as looking like "a giant crossword". Why is this, do you suppose?

    A   the sun made dark patches on the fields
    B   the hedges dividing the fields made them look like squares
    C   the fields were divided by square hedges
    D   the fields were numbered in squares

Fourth Passage

16   The Public Libraries referred to in the text offer

    A   opportunities for students to attend Further Education classes
    B   opportunities for students to further their studies
    C   assistance towards the maintenance of students in the London Borough Councils
    D   assistance to students who work in their local council

17   From the information given we understand that students

    A   may only borrow books from their local library
    B   must have special tickets to borrow books from another library
    C   may lend their tickets to students in other libraries
    D   may use their tickets to borrow books from other libraries

18   One of the main functions of the Reference Department is to

    A   consult students on the books required for their studies
    B   provide work for students on the premises
    C   provide books for students to consult
    D   counsel students on the books required for their studies

19   In order to help students further, a system exists whereby

    A   books on certain subjects can be borrowed from specialist libraries
    B   each library agrees to specialise in all subjects
    C   a group of libraries agree to specialise in one subject
    D   records are made of books on specialist subjects

20   The passage tells us that there is

    A   a central library in each area
    B   a library in the centre of each area
    C   one central library for all areas
    D   more than one central library in each area

PAPER 5: INTERVIEW (12 minutes)

Section A *Photograph*

Look at this photograph carefully and be prepared to answer some questions about it.

Describe the scene in this picture.

Why do you suppose the balloon is in a park?

What causes a balloon to float?

Would you like to go up in a balloon? Give your reasons.

1. Balloons as a means of transport.
2. Balloons as a successful media for advertising.
3. Possible dangers of ballooning.
4. An increasingly popular sport.

Section B *Topics*

Choose one of the following topics and prepare to give your views on it, for
1½ to 2 minutes. You may make notes, but do not try to write out a whole speech.

1   The hazards of smoking and why it is difficult to stop.

2   The main causes of strikes in present-day industry.

3   The value of youth hostelling to young people.

Section C *Dialogue*

(Prepare yourself to read the part of the HISTORY STUDENT. Your
Teacher will read the part of the Science Student.)

HISTORY STUDENT: Do you believe in ghosts?

Science Student: Of course not!

HISTORY STUDENT: I don't mean phantoms stalking the battlements with
their heads under their arms, or nuns moaning in
corridors or anything like that. No, I mean just that
feeling that there's someone there, an unidentified
presence –

Science Student: Isn't that what they call E.S.P.?

HISTORY STUDENT: Extra Sensory Perception? Perhaps that's what it is.
I know I've felt it when I've been terribly worried or
depressed. Once or twice I think I've even seen something, a sort of benign influence –

Science Student: Alcoholic influence, you mean. Anyone could see
things on the amount of beer you put away.

HISTORY STUDENT: Oh, do be serious for a minute. What I'm trying to
say is I've always been slightly psychic. When I was a
child I was – well – different, I suppose – hypersensitive
to atmosphere. I can still remember screaming my
head off the first time I was taken to the swimming
baths.

Science Student: I can't see what that's got to do with being hypersensitive – cold feet, more likely.

HISTORY STUDENT: Oh, really! Here am I trying to have an interesting
discussion and you persist in being frivolous. All I can
say is, you'd better watch out or when I die I shall
come back and haunt you!

Science Student: That won't be much use. I don't believe in ghosts.
Remember?

Section D *Situations*

1 You are in a restaurant having lunch when you discover you have left your wallet at home. Call the Manager and explain.

2 You are on holiday with a friend who proves to be very lax about paying his share of the expenses. Speak to him about this, explaining why you find it unsatisfactory.

3 You are in England and want to take something typically English back to your family, but you cannot afford a great deal. Go to a gift shop and ask for advice.

4 You bought an expensive sweater at a high class store and, after one washing, it has shrunk. Take it back and complain.

5 You are having difficulty in completing an application form for a job. Ask a friend for help.

TEST FIVE

Answer questions 1, 2 and 3. You should spend about the same amount of time on each.

Section A

1. Either (*a*) Methods of predicting the future – discuss.

or (*b*) Sounds and smells – the memories they evoke.

2. Either (*a*) The Death Penalty – is it ever justified?

or (*b*) "All power corrupts." Comment on this statement.

Section B

3. Read the following passage and then answer the questions that follow it.

IDLENESS

It has always been a mystery to me why idleness should be considered the prerogative of the rich. The phrase "the idle rich" carries with it an aura of stately homes, wild parties and yachts on the Mediterranean. Yet most of the really rich people one reads about are exceptionally hard-working. It stands to
5 reason, since acquiring wealth and managing to hang on to it in the modern world demands a high degree of ingenuity, manipulation and commercial expertise. To remain rich a man may have to form himself into a limited company, must keep a vigilant eye on the stock market, must gauge to a nicety the exact moment for investing in a Picasso or a decorative wife – never by any
10 stretch of the imagination can he be termed "idle". He cannot afford to be.

The poor on the other hand are notoriously diligent and deserving, taking pride in such phrases as "sweated labour," and, the women in particular, "working their fingers to the bone" to support equally work-conscious families. The very concept that the poor are idle is obnoxious. A tramp sleeping on a
15 park bench is not "idle" but "socially deprived," a gang of teenagers terrorising an old lady or bashing up a telephone box are "under-privileged" – poor, maybe, but never idle.

Who then are the truly idle? Neither rich nor poor, but the lovers of idleness for its own sake. Poets and dreamers perhaps, and those dedicated idlers who
20 will devote hours to the contemplation of the industrious ant, the passage of the clouds or the changing faces of the sea. There is a story, by G. K. Chesterton I think, of a man suspected of a crime because he was unable to prove that he was doing nothing at the time. Suspicion lifted, however, when it was learnt that he

was a poet – a class of persons naturally expected to be idle while others go about
25 their daily business. This to me is the very essence of idleness: to thoroughly
enjoy doing nothing while everyone else is doing something.

(*a*) How does the author compare the theme of idleness in the first and second
     paragraphs?

(*b*) Comment on the author's use of irony in the second paragraph.

(*c*) Explain the distinction between "under-privileged" and "socially
     deprived". (Paragraph 2)

(*d*) Why does the author use the expression "bashing up a telephone box"
     instead of "damaging a telephone box"?

(*e*) Comment on the contrast between "dedicated idlers" and "the industrious
     ant". (Paragraph 3)

(*f*) Why does the writer use the phrase "a class of persons" when referring to
     poets?

(*g*) In what way is the reference to the story by G. K. Chesterton amusing in
     connection with the theme of idleness?

PAPER 2: READING COMPREHENSION (1¼ hours)

Section A

Choose the word or phrase which best completes each sentence. **Give one
answer only** to each question.

1 The accounts show a _____ of £200 this month.
   A decrease   B devaluation   C deficit   D divergence
   E deterioration

2 At first the Council refused to enlarge the playground, but this decision
  was _____ revised.
   A after   B following   C next   D subsequently
   E successively

3 Will you pay cash for the goods, madam, or would you like them _____ to
  your account?
   A charged   B paid   C priced   D indebted   E receipted

4 The Housing Committee has decided to give _____ to young married
  couples with children.
   A presentation   B preferment   C prestige   D priority
   E prescription

5 I don't _____ to know much about Art, but I know what I like.
   A believe   B pretend   C imagine   D represent   E assert

6   Arthur Brown has always been _____ supporter of his local football team.
    A   an unyielding   B   a staunch   C   a forcible   D   a sure
    E   an unbeaten

7   Owing to the rise in the cost of petrol, I am thinking of _____ in a bicycle.
    A   profiting   B   circulating   C   expending   D   capitalising
    E   investing

8   The local authority are proposing to make severe _____ in their educational budget.
    A   holes   B   cuts   C   gashes   D   gaps   E   rents

9   It is _____ we did something about redecorating the sitting-room.
    A   high time   B   long time   C   good time   D   full-time
    E   half-time

10 There is a sale at Hamfridge's next week with _____ in all departments.
    A   redundancies   B   decreases   C   reductions   D   debasements
    E   deferments

11 My mother is so _____ that she believes everything she is told.
    A   credulous   B   credible   C   believable   D   undoubted
    E   creditable

12 This drawer is _____. You will have to get something to break it open.
    A   impacted   B   fixed   C   rooted   D   jammed   E   set

13 That painting, believed to be by Rembrandt, has recently been proved to be a _____.
    A   falsehood   B   representation   C   forgery   D   deception
    E   pretence

14 John, who is an orphan, is being brought up by _____ parents.
    A   substitute   B   foster   C   deputy   D   secondary
    E   adoptive

15 Before you decide to buy that house, you ought to have it _____.
    A   overlooked   B   observed   C   scanned   D   calculated
    E   surveyed

16 George Hopkins is not the owner of "The George and Dragon" public house, he is only the _____.
    A   holder   B   employer   C   licenser   D   licensee   E   consigner

17 Although her marriage was very unhappy, Mrs Stephens remained with her husband for the _____ of the children.
    A   care   B   sake   C   aid   D   cause   E   reason

18 To everyone's relief, the lost children were found _____ on the mountainside.
    A   sweet and low   B   high and mighty   C   hard and fast
    D   safe and sound   E   in and out

19 The Company could not meet its liabilities and was obliged to go into _____.
    A   liquidation   B   dissolution   C   distribution   D   abolition
    E   nullification

20 The expedition has left for the Andes and there is no _____ when it will return.
    A informing   B reporting   C knowing   D advising
    E detailing

21 Albert Harris is going to _____ the question of rubbish disposal at our next Residents Association meeting.
    A lift   B raise   C rise   D arouse   E lay

22 Our villa in Spain is on the top of a hill overlooking some olive _____.
    A gardens   B orchards   C fields   D groves   E meadows

23 The _____ of juvenile crime has increased by ten per cent in our neighbourhood.
    A rate   B happening   C event   D occasion   E occurrence

24 During the summer vacation, Peter worked as _____ labourer for a building firm.
    A an informal   B an impermanent   C an accidental
    D an unstable   E a casual

25 The people in the mountain village had no warning of the _____ avalanche.
    A impending   B converging   C arriving   D following
    E succeeding

26 As a child, Mozart was considered to be an infant _____.
    A fantasy   B miracle   C spectacle   D prodigy
    E sensation

27 The sea was so rough that the little boat _____.
    A capsized   B inverted   C sagged   D bent   E reversed

28 The chances of meeting a tiger in Piccadilly Circus are about a million _____.
    A at one   B for one   C to one   D against one   E in one

29 After the snowstorm the road to Edinburgh was found to be _____.
    A impermeable   B impregnable   C impassable
    D imperceptible   E impressionable

30 The reviews of Hugo's new book were so insulting that I'm surprised he took them _____.
    A lying down   B standing up   C sitting down   D lying still
    E standing still

31 Mary can't play with the children next door because she is still in _____ for measles.
    A confinement   B detention   C internment   D seclusion
    E quarantine

32 The price of fresh fruit usually _____ according to the season.
    A vacillates   B fluctuates   C alternates   D oscillates
    E variegates

33 After considering the case, the judge put the young offender _____ for a year.
    A on trial   B on probation   C in restraint   D in control
    E in charge

34   I think I can say, without _____ myself, that I speak very good English.
     A   falsifying   B   exaggerating   C   magnifying   D   enhancing
     E   flattering

35   This photograph is rather _____ because my camera was out of focus.
     A   faded   B   blotted   C   spotted   D   blurred   E   smeared

36   What _____ have the Health Authorities taken to prevent the epidemic
     spreading?
     A   steps   B   plans   C   cares   D   grounds   E   stands

37   It was feared that the torrential rain would cause the river _____ its banks.
     A   to snap   B   to crack   C   to smash   D   to burst
     E   to crush

38   The accident was caused by the car _____ on an oily patch on the road.
     A   skidding   B   skimming   C   deviating   D   diverging
     E   sidling

39   The plot of this play is so absurd, it _____ on the ridiculous.
     A   touches   B   borders   C   edges   D   urges   E   hangs

40   The leaders of the two main political parties will meet each other _____ in
     a television interview next Wednesday.
     A   eye to eye   B   face to face   C   ear to ear   D   back to front
     E   back to back

Section B

In this section you will find after each of the passages a number of questions
or unfinished statements about the passage, each with four different ways of
finishing it. You must choose the one which you think fits best. **Give one answer
only** to each question.

First Passage

In a bay near Almeria in Southern Spain will be built the world's first underwater residence for tourists. The hotel will be 40 feet down in the Mediterranean.
As all the world opened to tour operators, there was still a frontier behind which
lay three quarters of the globe's surface, the sea; in whose cool depths light
5 fades; no winds blow; there are no stars. There even the most bored travellers
could recapture their sense of romance, terror or beauty. For a submerged
hotel is such a beautiful idea.
     The hotel will cost £170,000 and will be able to accommodate up to ten people
a night. Up until now only scientists and professional divers have lived under
10 the sea, but soon, for the first time, the public will be able to go down into the
darkness. They will have to swim down in diving suits, but at 40 feet there
would be no problem about decompression.
     Design of the hotel was crucial. Most of the underwater structures used be-
fore had been in the shape of a diving bell or submarine. Professional divers
15 could cope with such things but ordinary people would run the risk of violent
claustrophobia. Then an Austrian architect had the idea of making three inter-
connecting circular structures, 18 feet in diameter, and looking much like
flying saucers. They would be cast in concrete and launched from the shore.

Towed into position they would then be sunk. A foundation of cast concrete
20 would already be in place on the sea-bed. Pylons would attach the structures to
this. Once in position the structures would be pumped dry. The pylons, made
to withstand an uplift pressure of 350 tons, would then take the strain.

Cables linking the underwater structures to the hotel on shore would connect
it with electricity, fresh water, television, and an air pump, and also dispose
25 of sewage. Entry would be from underneath, up a ladder; because of the pressure
inside there would be no need of airlocks or doors.

The first structure would include a changing room and a shower area, where
the divers would get out of their gear. There would also be a kitchen and a
lavatory. The second structure would contain a dining room/lecture theatre,
30 and sleeping accommodation for eight people. The third structure would contain two suites. A steward would come down with the ten customers, to cook and
look after them. Television monitors would relay all that went on to the shore
so that discussions on the sea bed could be transmitted to all the world.

Around the hotel there are plans to build a strange secret garden, over 100
35 yards square, of plastic shapes, curves, circles, hollows. This would have a dual
function. First, to attract fish who would see it as a shelter and hiding place;
secondly, to allow guests looking out of the reinforced windows to see a
teeming underwater life.

So far at the site a diving tower 33 feet deep has been installed for diving
40 instruction. An aquarium has been built, and zoologists from Vienna University are in regular attendance to supervise its stocking. There are storage cup-
boards full of the plastic shapes for the underwater garden and there is a model
of the hotel. All that is needed now is permission from the Spanish Government
to start building.

41　From the passage we understand that tour operators were particularly
　　interested in the siting of the hotel as

　　A　it was still undiscovered
　　B　it was still unexplored
　　C　it would offer new possibilities
　　D　it would have unchanging weather

42　To reach the hotel the guests will have to

　　A　be champion swimmers
　　B　have scientific knowledge
　　C　be experienced divers
　　D　have special equipment

43　What design was finally considered most suitable for the new hotel?

　　A　three separate circles
　　B　three linked discs
　　C　three connected globes
　　D　three interlocked cylinders

44　In order for the hotel to be placed in the correct position under the sea it
　　would have to be

　　A　lowered down
　　B　dragged down
　　C　tugged down
　　D　hauled down

45 The hotel would be able to float under water because it would be

A   made of light material
B   350 tons in weight
C   filled with air
D   attached to pylons

46 It would not be necessary for the hotel to have doors because of the

A   shape of the rooms
B   position of the entrance
C   force of the air inside
D   force of the water outside

47 It is planned that sleeping quarters will be provided for the guests in the

A   second structure
B   second and third structures
C   first and third structures
D   third structure

48 The purpose of television monitors under the sea would be to relay

A   instructions from the sea bed to the shore
B   news from the shore to the sea bed
C   information from the world to the sea bed
D   information to the world from the sea bed

49 One of the reasons for building a hotel garden would be to

A   entertain the guests
B   hide the fish
C   experiment with new shapes
D   cultivate underwater plants

50 In the passage we are told that zoologists came from Vienna University to

A   study the fish in the aquarium
B   decide which fish to put in the aquarium
C   supervise the building of the aquarium
D   help build the aquarium

Second Passage

My first visit to Paris began in the company of some earnest students. My friend and I, therefore, being full of independence and the love of adventure, decided to go off on our own and explore Northern France as hitch-hikers.

We managed all right down the main road from Paris to Rouen, because there
5   were lots of vegetable trucks with sympathetic drivers. After that we still made headway along secondary roads to Fécamp, because we fell in with two family men who had left their wives behind and were off on a spree on their own. In Fécamp, having decided that it was pointless to reserve money for emergencies such as railway fares, we spent our francs in great contentment, carefully
10   arranging that we should have just enough left for supper and an overnight stay at the Youth Hostel in Dieppe, before catching the early morning boat.

Dieppe was only fifty miles away, so we thought it would be a shame to leave Fécamp until late in the afternoon.

There is a hill outside Fécamp, a steep one. We walked up it quite briskly,
15 saying to each other as the lorries climbed past us, that, after all, we couldn't
expect a French truck driver to stop on a hill for us. It would be fine going from
the top.

It probably would have been fine going at the top, if we had got there before
the last of the evening truck convoy had passed on its way westwards along the
20 coast. We failed to realise that at first, and sat in dignified patience on the crest
of the hill. We were sitting there two and a half hours later – still dignified, but
less patient. Then we went about two hundred yards further down to a little
bistro, to have some coffee and ask advice from the proprietor. He told us that
there would be no more trucks and explained that our gentlemanly signalling
25 stood not the slightest chance of stopping a private motorist.

"This is the way one does it!" he exclaimed, jumping into the centre of the
road and completely barring the progress of a vast, gleaming car which con-
tained a rather supercilious Belgian family, who obviously thought nothing at
all of two bedraggled English students. However, having had to stop, they let us
30 into the back seat, after carefully removing all objects of value, including their
daughter.

Conversation was not easy, but we were more than content to stay quiet –
until the car halted suddenly in an out-of-the-way village far from the main
road, and we learned to our surprise that the Belgians went no farther. They left
35 us standing disconsolate on a deserted country road, looking sorrowfully after
them as their rear lamp disappeared into the darkness.

We walked in what we believed to be the general direction of Dieppe for a
long time. At about 11 p.m. we heard, far in the distance, a low-pitched staccato
rumbling. We ran to a rise in the road and from there we saw, as if it were some
40 mirage, a vast French truck approaching us. It was no time for half measures.
My friend sat down by the roadside and hugged his leg, and looked as much like
a road accident as nature and the circumstances permitted. I stood in the middle
of the road and held my arms out. As soon as the lorry stopped we rushed to
either side and gabbled out a plea in poor if voluble French for a lift to Dieppe.
45 There were two aboard, the driver and his relief, and at first they thought we
were a hold-up. When we got over that, they let us in, and resumed the journey.

We reached the Youth Hostel at Dieppe at about 1.30 a.m., or, as my friend
pointed out, precisely $3\frac{1}{2}$ hours after all doors had been locked. This, in fact, was
not true, because after we had climbed over a high wall and tip-toed across the
50 forecourt, we discovered that the door to the washroom was not properly
secured, and we were able to make our stealthy way to the men's dormitory
where we slept soundly until roused at 9.30 the following morning.

51 The author and his friend decided to hitch-hike together in Northern
   France as

   A   the other students didn't want to go with them
   B   it was difficult to find public transport
   C   they didn't want to stay with the other students
   D   it had never been explored

52 The travellers were able to reach Fécamp by getting a lift from

   A   two men who had left their wives
   B   two different lorry drivers
   C   two men driving different cars
   D   two men without their wives

53   Why did they spend most of their money in Fécamp?

    A   they saw no reason to save it
    B   the fares to Dieppe were very cheap
    C   they knew there would be no emergencies
    D   they were leaving early next morning

54   Why did they find it difficult to get a lift from Fécamp?

    A   the town was built on top of a hill
    B   they didn't reach the top of the hill early enough
    C   the lorries didn't stop at the top of the hill
    D   they couldn't stop the lorries at the top of the hill

55   The bistro proprietor thought that cars wouldn't stop for the two students because

    A   only gentlemen could understand their signals
    B   they only signalled to gentlemen
    C   they were too polite to signal
    D   their signals were too polite

56   The Belgian family made their daughter sit in the front of the car because they thought

    A   the students were too dirty to sit near
    B   the students wouldn't value her enough
    C   the students couldn't be trusted near her
    D   the students were too rude to speak to

57   Why were the two students surprised to see the lorry?

    A   It seemed to be coming from Dieppe
    B   No French lorries run at night
    C   It was late for a lorry to be running
    D   The lorry appeared to be running late

58   The author's friend sat down at the side of the road because

    A   he was too tired to walk any further
    B   he had had an accident and hurt his leg
    C   he thought the lorry driver would see him clearly there
    D   he wanted to give the lorry driver a reason to stop

59   The two students asked the lorry driver for a lift in

    A   rapid and accurate French
    B   slow and imprecise French
    C   quick and inaccurate French
    D   hesitant and precise French

60   The two friends were able to get inside the Youth Hostel as

    A   not all the doors were locked
    B   they managed to scale a wall
    C   they crossed a courtyard unobserved
    D   they entered the dormitory noiselessly

PAPER 3: USE OF ENGLISH (3 hours)

SECTION A

1. Fill each of the blanks in the passage with **one** suitable word.

The problem of adult illiteracy is _____(1) rise to considerable _____(2). The number of young people who leave school without the _____(3) to read is rapidly _____(4). It would seem that if urgent _____(5) are not taken to _____(6) this situation, we shall soon be living _____(7) a population _____(8) to that of the Middle _____(9) when only a small proportion of ordinary people were _____(10). The question is where the fault _____(11). Is there something _____(12) wrong with modern teaching _____(13) in our _____(14) schools? Are the classes too large for the teacher to _____(15) with, so that the _____(16) learner does not get the required _____(17) and so gives up trying, or do the modern media of television, radio and films make it unnecessary for the modern child to _____(18) to learn to read? _____(19) the reasons, the urgency of the problem should not be _____(20) if educational standards are to be maintained.

2. Finish each of the following sentences in such a way that it means exactly the same as the sentence printed before it.

Example: What was the staff's reaction to the Manager's resignation?

Answer: How *did the staff react to the Manager's resignation?*

He suffers very greatly, but he never complains.

1 However ....

The Government's decision to reduce Family Allowances is giving rise to considerable anxiety.

2   Considerable anxiety ....

The raising of the school-leaving age has resulted in unforeseen difficulties.

3   The difficulties ....

Do you agree with the Council's plans to widen the High Street?

4   Are you...

Don't repeat this to anyone, but Sanderson has been sacked.

5   Don't let ....

What are your views on Capital Punishment?

6   How ....?

I can't believe Councillor Bates really means to resign.

7   I find ....

My knowledge of mediaeval art is very limited.

8   I don't ....

It is impossible to prove that Louis was in the flat on the night of the murder.

9   There...

The value of this Roman coin is about £100.

10   This Roman coin...

3. Fill each of the numbered blanks with a suitable word or phrase.

Example: "I shan't be home till very late to-night."
            "Oh, then I *won't wait* up for you."

1   I don't think I should have told him even if he .... me.

2   **John:**   "How long have you been in England?"
    Maria: "Since September."
    John: "Oh, so by Christmas you ....here three months."

3   Will you please .... your radio, I'm trying to do my homework.

4   I'm so sorry to .... waiting, I was delayed on the Underground.

5   You .... Mary's face when I told her what Alan had said about her.

6   How many times .... you not to telephone me at the office?

7   **Susan:** Are you very busy?
    Ann: Not particularly.
    Susan: Then do you think you.............................the ironing for me?

8   **Peter:** What have you done to your hair?
    Alice: I've had it cut.
    Peter: Well, I think it .... long.

9   You .... a cake, I made one this morning.

10 If Dr Ferguson telephones, tell him I .... him tomorrow about ten.

4. For each of the sentences below, write a sentence **as similar as possible in meaning to the original** sentence, but using the word given in capital letters.

Example: I don't want to discuss the matter.
          RATHER

Answer: *I would rather not discuss the matter.*
          ....

1   The child's illness has been caused by malnutrition.
    RESULT

    ....

2   It never occurred to me that Simon was married.
    IDEA

    ....

3   I think you have made those curtains too long.
    SHORTEN

    ....

4 The final score in the match between Derby County and Queen's Park Rangers on Saturday was one all.
DREW

....

5 The Masons' house must have doubled its value since they bought it.
TWICE

....

6 John tells me he has entered for the Interpreters' Examination next June.
SITTING

....

7 The local Council have abandoned their scheme for building a shopping precinct on the new housing estate.
DROP

....

8 It is quite unnecessary to take all those clothes for a camping holiday.
POINT

....

9 The plans for the construction of the new motorway have not yet been published.
SECRET

....

10 We know the kind of house we want, all that remains is to find the money.
QUESTION

....

SECTION B

5. Read the following passage, and then answer the questions which follow it.

THE QUALITIES TO LOOK FOR IN A WIFE

Chastity, perfect modesty in word, deed, and even thought is so essential that without it, no female is fit to be a wife. It is not enough that a young woman should abstain from anything approaching boldness in her behaviour towards men; it is not enough that she casts down her eyes, or turns aside her head with
5 a smile, when she hears an indelicate allusion: she ought to appear not to understand it, and to receive from it no more impression than if she were a post. A loose woman is a disagreeable acquaintance: what must she be then, as a wife? Your "free and hearty" girls I have liked very much to talk and laugh

with; but never, for one moment, did it enter my mind that I could have endured
10 a "free and hearty" girl for a wife. A wife, I repeat, is to last for life, she is to be
a counterbalance to troubles and misfortune: and therefore must be perfect.

Sobriety. By the word "sobriety," in a young woman, I mean a great deal
more than a rigid abstinence from the love of drink; I mean sobriety of conduct.
The word "sober" does not confine itself to matters of drink: it expresses steadi-
15 ness, seriousness, carefulness, scrupulous propriety of conduct. Now sobriety
is a great qualification in the person you mean to make your wife. Playful,
frivolous, careless girls are very amusing, and they may become sober, but you
have no certainty of this. To be sure, when girls are mere children they should
play and romp like children, but when they arrive at that age when they begin
20 to think of managing a house, then it is time for them to cast away the levity of
the child.

If any young man imagines that this sobriety of conduct in young women
must be accompanied by seriousness approaching gloom, he is, according to my
experience, very much deceived. The contrary is the fact; for I have found that
25 gay and laughing women are the most insipid of souls and are generally down in
the dumps. A greater curse than a wife of this description it would be somewhat
difficult to find. I hate a dull, melancholy thing: I could not have existed in the
same house with such a thing for a single month. Whereas a sober woman is
underneath joyful and contented.

30 Industry. By industry, I do not mean merely labour or activity of the body,
for purposes of gain or of saving; for there may be industry amongst those who
have more money than they know what to do with. Industry in the wife is always
necessary to the happiness and prosperity of the family. If she is lazy then the
children will be lazy: everything, however urgent, will be put off to the last
35 moment, then it will be done badly, and in many cases, not at all: the dinner
will be late, the journey or visit will be delayed; inconveniences of all sorts will
be continually arising: there will always be a heavy arrear of things unperformed;
and therefore a lazy woman must always be a curse.

Finally beauty . . . the last in point of importance. But the great use of female
40 beauty, the great practical advantage of it, is that it naturally and unavoidably
tends to keep the husband in a good humour with himself, to make him pleased
with his bargain. Beauty is, in some degree, a matter of taste, what one man
admires, another does not; and it is fortunate for us that it is so. But still there
are certain things that all men admire; and a husband is always pleased when
45 he perceives that a portion, at least, of these things are in his own possession: he
takes his possession as a compliment to himself: there must have been, he thinks,
some charm, seen or unseen, to have caused him to be blessed with such an
acquisition.

1 The author thinks that to be a good wife, a woman should ....

....

2 When is it a good time for girls to start acting in a mature way? ....

....

3 Why is industry important in a wife? ....

....

7 What is a "free and hearty" girl? (l. 8) ....

....

8 "To be sober" does not always mean the opposite of being drunk – what else can it mean? ....

....

9 What is the "levity of the child"? (ll. 20–21) ....

....

10 Which of the following best explains the use of "gloom"? (l. 23) darkness/ despondency/wretchedness/dimness/obscurity ....

11 The phrase "down in the dumps" means (ll. 25–26) ....

....

12 Why does the author choose to use the words "joyful" and "contented" (l. 29) in connection with a sober wife? ....

....

13 What aspects of a "lazy" (l. 33) woman's behaviour does the author consider reprehensible? ....

....

14 What does the author mean by "to make him pleased with his bargain"? (ll. 41–42) ....

....

15 "Beauty is . . . a matter of taste" (l. 42) because ....

....

16 What is "an acquisition" referred to in ll. 47–48? ....

....

17 What does a husband consider "caused him to be blessed with such an acquisition"? (ll. 47–48) ....

....

18 In a paragraph of not more than 100 words describe what the author considers necessary qualities to look for in a wife.

....

....

....

....

....

....

....

....

....

....

SECTION C

6. You are a Youth Leader at a Youth Club in an overcrowded neighbourhood with poor amenities. You have decided to enlist the support of some of the more responsible members to prevent the theft and vandalism that has been occurring on the Club premises. Begin your talk as follows and write another 125–175 words.

"Well, boys, no prizes for guessing why I suggested this little get-together. You don't need me to tell you what's been going on lately – the smashing up of the gym gear for instance ....

PAPER 4: LISTENING COMPREHENSION (40 minutes)

The passages on which these questions are based will be found in the Appendix.

First Passage

1 What is the most puzzling feature of the incidents that have occurred in the Bermuda Triangle area?

   A The unexplained wreckage found in the area
   B The lack of evidence of disaster
   C The appearance of the wreckage
   D The disastrous losses in the area

2 Before contact with missing aircraft has been lost

   A unidentified signals have sometimes been received
   B confusing signals have sometimes been received
   C the pilot has invariably reported bad weather conditions
   D the pilot has never made any request for assistance

3 The five United States Navy planes that disappeared were

   A trying to locate a missing plane
   B trying to rescue a plane in trouble
   C on a special mission
   D on a normal flight

4 The curious white lights observed on the surface of the sea in the Bermuda Triangle area

   A were only seen by astronauts
   B were unearthed by Columbus
   C were seen from a spacecraft
   D were not discovered for five centuries

5 The cause of the disappearances of ships and planes in the area is

   A known only to laymen
   B inexplicable to scientists
   C known only to scientists
   D comprehensible only to scientists

Second Passage

6 From the passage it would seem that most admirers of Frances Fanshawe's books are

   A commissioned in the armed services
   B employed in the Secret Service
   C over twenty-five years old
   D hoping to make their fortunes

7   Which of the following statements best describes Captain Peters?

   A   He closely resembles Sherlock Holmes
   B   He is never at a loss
   C   He has extra-sensory powers
   D   He has superhuman strength

8   In Frances Fanshawe's book "Murder on the Moon" the Earth is about to be destroyed by

   A   the power of an unknown force
   B   an unnamed source of energy
   C   an association of unworldly business men
   D   the machinations of big business men

9   Readers of "Murder on the Moon" may be puzzled to decide how Captain Peters

   A   dressed himself as an astronaut
   B   became proficient in space travel
   C   managed to journey to the Moon
   D   discovered the plotters on Earth

10   Among the adventures described in the book, one of the most exciting is

   A   a chase in a moon-crater
   B   a fight on the edge of a crater
   C   the hijacking of a woman astronaut
   D   the disappearance of a space machine

Third Passage

11   This announcement informs Members of the Eastchester Historical Association that they

   A   will be expected to spend a day on a visit to a place of interest
   B   are invited to make a visit to a place of interest
   C   are expected to make their own arrangements for Tuesday, September 14th
   D   should arrange to be free on Tuesday, September 14th

12   We understand that the Godfrey Tea-Rooms are situated

   A   within easy reach of Godfrey's Grave
   B   at a considerable distance from Godfrey's Grave
   C   adjoining a small public car park
   D   at the foot of a precipitous hill

13   Although George Godfrey did not die on the date that he had predicted, he

   A   was not surprised that his prediction had been inaccurate
   B   was not surprised that the planets had altered their courses
   C   believed that his original prediction had been accurate
   D   believed he had altered the course of the planets

14   Visitors to Godfrey's Grave will discover that the roof is

    A   arched to represent the sky
    B   arched in the shape of a star
    C   painted with twelve stars
    D   dedicated to astrological signs

15   From what we are told it would seem that opinion on the architectural beauty of Godfrey's Grave is

    A   more or less in agreement
    B   under constant review
    C   universally critical
    D   strongly divided

Fourth Passage

16   It would seem that the discussion in which Rosa and Andrew were involved

    A   had started an hour before they left on their journey
    B   had started after they had left on their journey
    C   had continued uninterrupted since they arrived at the hotel
    D   had first arisen as they got off the train

17   With regard to matters of importance Andrew believed that women were

    A   only capable of arguing on an empty stomach
    B   only capable of arguing on tea and aspirins
    C   capable of arguing on only tea and aspirins
    D   incapable of arguing on a full stomach

18   Why do you think that Andrew did not welcome the idea of a day trip to France?

    A   he disliked going on day trips
    B   he was afraid he might be sea-sick
    C   he had not enough money to pay for the trip
    D   he disliked going to foreign places

19   How had Rosa first learned about the steamer trips to France?

    A   they had been advertised on a station platform
    B   they had been advertised by a station announcer
    C   she had seen a poster about them in the train
    D   she had heard an announcement about them on the train

20   As far as the holiday in general was concerned, Andrew was suffering from a sense of inferiority because

    A   he hadn't borrowed enough money to cover his expenses
    B   he had had to borrow money to pay Rosa's expenses
    C   Rosa had had to lend him money to pay his expenses
    D   he was unable to pay more than his own expenses

PAPER 5: INTERVIEW (12 minutes)

Section A *Photograph*

Look at this photograph carefully and be prepared to answer some questions about it.

Describe the scene in the picture.
What are the horses wearing?
Why is one of the men walking behind?
What occasion do you think this is?

Methods of ploughing in candidate's country.
Ecological advantage of horse-drawn ploughs.
Farming as a career. Disadvantages and advantages of working on the land.
Mechanisation of farming equipment – good or bad.

Section B *Topics*

Choose one of the following topics and prepare to give your views on it, for 1½ to 2 minutes. You may make notes, but do not try to write out a whole speech.

1   Husbands and wives who both work should share domestic chores.

2   The purpose of education is to adapt the child to his social environment.

3   Material success rarely brings happiness.

Section C *Dialogue*

(Prepare yourself to read the part of the HUSBAND. The teacher will read the other part.)

HUSBAND: Shall I turn the telly on?

Wife: What's on?

HUSBAND: Rather an interesting discussion on Race Relations – it should be good. There's been a lot of controversy about it lately.

Wife: Oh, I don't want to watch that. Much too boring.

HUSBAND: Boring? Don't you ever want to watch anything that makes you think? There are tremendous problems in the world in which we're all vitally involved – things that may ultimately affect the whole of humanity – and you find them boring!

Wife: I'm tired at the end of the day. I want to be entertained.

HUSBAND: Tired! You spend your whole day occupying yourself with trivialities – cooking, washing up, doing the household chores. You never exercise your mental faculties. If you're not careful, you'll be nothing but an animated vegetable by the time you're forty.

Wife: I rather like vegetables.

HUSBAND: Now you're just being facetious which, incidentally, is the lowest form of humour an intelligent person can stoop to. I suppose you want to watch the Old Time Music Hall with all those senile comedians trotting out their dreary old gags.

Wife: I don't particularly want to watch anything. I've got things to do actually.

HUSBAND: Things to do? But we haven't even had supper yet and I'm absolutely starving. I've only had a measly sandwich and a lager since breakfast –

Wife: That's just it. We must have supper now. I have to be at my Archaeology Class by 7.30.

HUSBAND: Archaeology Class? What use is that to you? Why don't you go to some decent cookery classes and learn how to cook something besides scrambled eggs and baked beans? You need to increase your range. What're we having tonight, by the way?

Wife: Er – scrambled egg and baked beans.

Section D *Situations*

1   You believe that one of your parents is seriously ill, but he/she refuses to see a doctor. Try to persuade him/her to do so.

2   Walking along a quiet street at night, you see a suspicious parcel outside the door of a bank. Telephone the Police and give details.

3   You have been offered promotion to another job in your company, but this will mean living abroad for at least three years. Refuse the offer and give your reasons for wishing to remain in your own country.

4   You have received an unpleasant letter from the Electricity Company demanding payment of a bill which you settled three weeks ago. Telephone the Electricity Company and demand an explanation.

5   You are collecting door to door for an old people's outing. Explain to a reluctant householder why it would be worth while making a donation.

APPENDIX

LISTENING COMPREHENSION

Passages

Four passages are given for each test. The questions on these passages will be found in the test. Each passage is read twice, with time allowed for the student to select and check his answers.

TEST ONE

First Passage

Two landscape painters stood at the window looking at the landscape which was also a seascape, and both were curiously impressed by it, though their impressions were not exactly the same. To one of them, who was a rising artist from London, it was new as well as strange. To the other, who was a local artist, but with something more than local celebrity, it was better known; but perhaps all the more strange for what he knew of it.

In terms of tone and form, as those men saw it, it was a stretch of sand against a stretch of sunset, the whole scene lying in strips of sombre colour, dead green and bronze and brown that were not merely dull but in that light in some way more mysterious than gold. All that broke these lovely lines was a long building which ran out from the fields into the sands of the sea, so that its fringe of dreary weeds and rushes seemed almost to meet the seaweed. But its most singular feature was that the upper part of it had the ragged outlines of a ruin, pierced by so many wide windows and large rents as to be a mere dark skeleton against the dying light; while the lower bulk of the building had hardly any windows at all, most of them being blind and bricked up and their outlines only faintly traceable in the twilight. But one of the bottom windows at least was still a window; and it seemed strangest of all that it showed a light.

"Who on earth can live in that old shell?" exclaimed the Londoner, who was a big, bohemian-looking man, young but with a shaggy red beard that made him look older. Chelsea knew him familiarly as Harry Payne.

"Ghosts, you might suppose," replied his friend Martin Wood, "well, the people who live there really are rather like ghosts."

Second Passage

Inspector Harrison, hunched with cold, and cursing as he plodded up the drive, heard the screams muffled through the fog. He began to run in the direction from which he fancied the sounds came. As he ran forward, he saw a black shape loom up in front of him in the drive. Perceiving it was a man, he took a running jump and caught hold of him by the collar. The figure uttered a cry and revealed itself as Constable Briggs.

Harrison wasted no words in apology. "Hear those screams? Where did they come from?"

"Down by the pond, I believe, sir," panted Briggs. "I was patrolling round the house when I heard splashing and running and then those screams. Made me feel quite funny."

"Come on," said Harrison curtly.

Briggs' sense of direction was good even in this fog, and in a few moments they half stumbled over a woman, who knelt moaning on the ground, the naked form of a boy half dragged across her lap.

Briggs picked the woman up bodily and Harrison flashed his torch on the boy now lying on the ground. Feeling his heart and satisfied that it was still faintly beating, he knelt down and applied artificial respiration for a few moments. Then, taking off his coat, he wrapped it round the boy and, lifting him up, swung him over his shoulder.

They made a painfully slow journey back to the house. As they stepped inside, the light temporarily blinded them, but the housekeeper who had been waiting, perplexed and anxious, in the shadow of the staircase, hurried to Harrison's side. With a little cry she took the boy from him and looked down into the ashen face of her own son.

Third Passage

It was growing dark when Stephen returned to Hollow Wood. A summer mist rising a few feet from the ground spread across the fields like a transparent wall, broken by scattered bars of light from the cottage windows. On such a night, so softly and treacherously damp, it would be an easy matter to catch a chill and find oneself in bed for a matter of days, he thought. It looked as though the fine weather was over for a while and though he had no wish to catch cold, he felt somehow relieved as though the heat had oppressed him without him being aware of it.

Inside the wood it was gloomy but still light enough to see. It did not take him long to find the patch of deadly nightshade he had noted earlier. He made a careful investigation and found, as he had expected, that a large number of the plants appeared to have been cut off with a knife or a pair of sharp scissors, and there were traces of footprints, as though whoever had gathered them had gone to some trouble to find the sturdier ones. He examined these footprints with care and came to the conclusion that someone had trampled on the undergrowth hereabouts, most probably a man. He thought at first that it might have been Francis Bracken, but could not be sure for the footprints suggested that they had been made by a pair of stout boots, and Francis did not wear boots. He remembered, too, that Francis, who was a nervous individual, seldom took the popular short cut through Hollow Wood to the village, since he had been threatened by a tramp who was making a temporary home there.

Fourth Passage

"The Cosmic Connection" by Carl Sagan

The author is an aggressive, brilliant and literate astronomer. This vastly entertaining book has a simple manner with complex ideas, without being patronising, and is often very funny.

In 274 pages Sagan deals with everything from the formation of the Earth to the puzzling possibilities of contact with extra-terrestial life. This is the moment in history when man's stepping into the Universe has suddenly become conceivable. To Sagan this is more exciting and important than was the exploration of the New World in the sixteenth century. So expenditure on the space programme, pruned of recent excesses, ought to continue – it is, according to Sagan, no larger a part of America's gross national income than was the relative cost to England in the sixteenth century of exploration in sailing ships.

The book is not for scientific illiterates, nor is Sagan a pedestrian scientist. Although he makes short work of the unidentified foreign objects (UFO) spotters, he is unafraid to take us on a speculative journey to a black hole which, for all he knows, might be the quick route to somewhere else, not necessarily our universe.

Sagan exhibits a passionate interest in life in the cosmos, in which there are almost certainly civilisations much more advanced than our own. We are the result of a number of relatively recent cosmic accidents, but for all that, Sagan is no less excited about our future.

TEST TWO

First Passage

Anderson could not remember that he had ever been in the room before, yet every detail was as familiar to him as if he had lived there all his life. The woman who had admitted him had asked him to wait while she went to inform her brother who, she said, was upstairs. Anderson was expected, she added, and would he make himself comfortable while he waited.

She left him standing in the poorly-lit high-ceilinged room with the curtains half drawn to keep out the night and the dust covers over the chairs. I know, he thought, without lifting the covers, exactly the pattern of the brocade on those chairs and one of them, that one by the fireplace, has a broken spring that digs uncomfortably into one's back when it is sat in. Without even looking, he could have given the names of the books on the shelves, knew that the little clock on the mantelpiece was permanently five minutes fast, and that if he pushed open the French windows, he could walk out on to a wide lawn with rose borders and a sundial whose markings had been almost obliterated by age.

The portraits on the wall were also familiar to him, yet nameless, like faces seen in a dream. They stared at him with sly, secret smiles, knowing and yet not known, and suddenly he was seized with an inward panic, a terrible realisation that he was no longer himself, Anderson, who had come to see over a house for sale, but that he had entered another identity, that he was, in fact, someone else, a stranger, about whose life he knew nothing yet to whom every object in that room touched some chord of recollection. He stood stock still, wanting to run away, to get back to sanity and his car, but lacking the power to move. The door opened behind him and a small, high-pitched voice said irritably, "So you've come at last. I must say you've been long enough about it."

Second Passage

I have always been attracted by people of unusual habits. By this I do not imply hippies and drop-outs or any one of that band of unhappy people for whom modern society is too sick and uncivilised to bear. No, I mean those quiet, orderly people, living apparently blameless lives, who enrich their humdrum existences by adopting odd quirks and passions, unlikely routines or harmless manias for useless objects. Like the bank clerk I know, who will not eat his breakfast toast, until the bread has been exposed to the early rays of the sun, and after that he toasts it on one side only. Since he lives in England enjoying only a reluctant sun, he is frequently breakfastless. Another couple I know, in all outward respects perfectly ordinary, are convinced that since Man was descended from the apes, he ought to live in a tree. They have a small neat bungalow in which they keep two dogs. a cat and a hamster, but they have built themselves living quarters among the branches of a large oak where they have lived happily for years much respected by the local community. I once had a secretary who collected earwigs, though what she did with them I never knew. They were kept in little boxes in her desk, and when they escaped, as they frequently did, she would be assiduous in collecting them from whatever part of the office they had chosen to wander. This idiosyncrasy did not affect her work – she was one of the best secretaries I ever had – and I believe that she loved them because they were small and thin like herself and had a way of scuttling about in very much the way she did. Life, I am sure, would be very much poorer without such people in it. Sometimes I feel I am lacking in personality, since I have none of these strange habits, unless you count the fact that I never eat eggs unless they are boiled in brandy.

Third Passage

He was not the old man you would have expected to see in an English first-class carriage, as first-class fares are so expensive, save that now in these democratic days you may see anyone anywhere. The old man, who was thin and wiry, had large shabby boots, loose and ancient trousers, a flopping garden straw hat. His hands were gnarled like the knots of trees. He was terribly clean. He had blue eyes. On his knees was a large basket and from this he ate his massive lunch – here an immense sandwich with enormous pieces of ham, there a colossal apple, a monstrous pear –

"Going far?" munched the old man.

"No," said Harkness blushing, "to Treliss. I change at Trewth, I believe. We should be there at 4.30."

"Should be," said the old man, dribbling through his pear. "The train's late . . . Another tourist," he added suddenly.

"I beg your pardon?" said Harkness.

"Another of these damned tourists. You are, I mean. I live at Treliss. Such as you drove me away."

"I am sorry," said Harkness, smiling faintly. "I suppose I am, if by tourist you mean somebody who is travelling to a place to see what it is like and enjoy its beauty. A friend has told me of it. He says it is the most beautiful place in England."

"Beauty," said the old man, licking his fingers – "a lot you tourists think about beauty – with your coaches and oranges and babies and Americans. If I had my way I'd make the Americans pay a tax, spoiling our country as they do."

"I am an American," said Harkness faintly.

The old man licked his thumb, looked at it, and licked it again. "I wouldn't have thought it," he said. "Where's your accent?"

"I have lived in this country a great many years off and on," Harkness explained, "and we don't all say 'I guess' every moment," he added smiling.

Smiling, yes. But how deeply he detested this unfortunate conversation. How happy he had been, and now this old man with his rudeness and his violence had smashed the peace into a thousand fragments. But the old man spoke little more. He only stared at Harkness out of his blue eyes, and said:

"Treliss is too beautiful a place for you. It will do you harm," and fell instantly asleep.

Fourth Passage

The chief claim to distinction of Shoreditch lies in the fact that the first theatres of London were built there in the seventeenth century.

The Shoreditch Theatre was the first real theatre to be built in England and was erected within the precincts of Holywell Priory, where the players were outside the jurisdiction of the Lord Mayor, for stage plays were forbidden. Companies of players, however, were springing up all over the country, generally under the protection of some nobleman. Amongst these were the Earl of Leicester's Servants, with James Burbage as their manager. Burbage borrowed £600 from his father-in-law and built the Shoreditch Theatre, a round wooden structure, which was afterwards carefully pulled down by his son Richard and re-erected in Southwark as the Globe. Richard was the original creator of most of Shakespeare's great characters, including Hamlet, and appears to have been one of the greatest actors on the English stage. The site of the Shoreditch Theatre has recently been determined by a careful survey and is found to have been partly on the site of a furniture factory at the corner of Curtain Road.

The Curtain was a rival theatre and was so named from the fact that it had a curtain which shut off the stage from the auditorium. This theatre had associations with Burbage and Green, players from the town of Stratford-upon-Avon, and later with the son of a Stratford butcher, who was a boy at school when the theatre was built. His name was William Shakespeare. He came to London as a young man and was employed at the Curtain in minor parts, but his chief work was adapting plays, from which he proceeded to writing them.

Not far away was another theatre, the Fortune, a property aptly named, for it was owned by Alleyn who made his money from it.

TEST THREE

First Passage

Where Joanna stood down by the water's edge, the sand lay soft and virgin, ruffled here and there into gentle ridges by the wind, unmarked by footprints or litter. It stretched in a great expanse of silver to the base of the cliffs, broken here and there by jagged grey rocks and clear sandy pools. Looking out to sea, Abbot's Island lay like a green finger at the entrance to the bay. Joanna wondered vaguely how long it would take to swim out there and whether the sea really covered it when the tide was right up, as she had been told. If so, it would make the navigation of even a small boat difficult unless one was familiar with the bay, for in spite of its serene appearance, the island extended below the water level in a reef of treacherous rocks. It's like a person you can't trust, thought Joanna, all smiles on the outside, so that you don't recognise the treachery until it's too late. Disquieted by these thoughts, she half turned away, but as she did so, she saw the figure of what seemed to be a man appear suddenly on the highest point of the island. He stood there like a great bird, flapping his arms as if they were wings. What was he doing? Signalling? Shouting for help? She strained her ears, trying to hear, but no sound was carried to her over the water. The strange, ungainly figure on the island continued to make swooping movements with his arms, and now he began to jump up and down as if he were performing some strange ritual dance of which only he knew the significance. This brought to mind some half-remembered story of the Abbot who had been drowned here centuries ago and whose ghost was said to haunt the island in times of danger. She bent down, hunted for her glasses in her beach bag and put them on to see better. When she looked up, the figure had disappeared. A grey cloud momentarily obscured the sun and above her she saw the white hovering wings of a giant seagull.

Second Passage

TYPEWRITING AND SECRETARIAL OPPORTUNITIES

We are a major company who are interested in recruiting school-leavers with or without previous typewriting and secretarial skills. If you have taken a typewriting or secretarial course at school or technical college, you can apply to go straight into our Typing Service or to be a trainee secretary. If you do not have these skills we will train you.

Each year we recruit girls for our part-time and full-time typing training courses. We expect applicants for this scheme to have reached G.C.E. Ordinary Pass Level in at least four subjects including English language. Those doing a part-time course work in departments as junior clerks and spend up to two hours a day in our Training Department for six to nine months. They then attend a five-week full time course to qualify for the Typing Service. Girls of 16–17 with very good examination results may be selected for our full-time typing courses. At the end of three months they are qualified typists and join our Typing Service.

When girls have gained sufficient copy typing experience they can gain promotion first to audio typist and later to audio secretarial posts.

We also recruit girls with two Advanced Level passes or equivalent for our full-time secretarial courses. They will spend three months in the Training Department learning shorthand and typing and other secretarial skills. This is followed by a period consolidating their technical skills and a further period in trainee secretarial positions during which time they put into practice what they have learned. Within a year most girls could expect to be in full secretarial positions, although promotion will depend upon an assessment of their secretarial skills.

Third Passage

Two British mountaineers have reached the summit of Mount Everest by its difficult south-west face. Dougal Haston of Edinburgh and Doug Scott of Nottingham became the first Britons to climb the 29,028 ft. mountain and the first climbers to scale the steep direct route up the south-west face.

In reaching the summit within five weeks of starting out, they are also thought to have climbed the mountain in record time.

The pair completed their climb at 6 p.m. local time on Wednesday and were well ahead of the schedule set by Chris Bonington, the leader of the expedition. This could give the opportunity for other climbers to reach the summit as the Himalayan winter weather is not expected to begin for at least another three weeks. Eight other climbers in the team are believed to be capable of reaching the top.

The expedition was the strongest to attempt the route, but the speed of their success has been remarkable. According to the original plan, the lead climbers were to attack the steep rock band, which juts from the face of the cliff at 26,500 ft. and has blocked five previous attempts, by a new route. This tactic was clearly successful. The final camp was established above this cliff, but still an arduous climb away from the summit.

The route to the top lay across a broad snowfield and into a gulley, to join up with the south-east ridge. This is the last section of the easier route from the south col climb by Sir Edmund Hillary and Tenzing in 1953.

Because of the thinness of the air and exposure to the treacherous high level winds, the south-west face was regarded as the greatest challenge in mountaineering.

Fourth Passage

The Police Station at Brightstone Beach proved to be an old coastguard's cottage perched at the summit of such a steep and forbidding cliff that Charles was sweating before he had covered half the distance. As it happened Sergeant Beckett was some two hundred yards distant from his house engaged in some business with a shrimping net on the other side of the cliff where the sand was white like sugar. He was a large dreamy man with the face of a saint and the instincts of a hermit-crab. In earlier life much of his energy had been devoted towards securing for himself the opportunity to lead a peaceful existence, combined with a little fishing, in the afternoon of his days. To this end he had conscientiously declined to shine at his duties save in one respect. He had accumulated an astonishing fund of information on the characteristics, natural and physical, of his native Brightstone Beach, to say nothing of an uncanny insight into the private lives of its inhabitants. It was not surprising, therefore, that he was considered an excellent man for the appointment when it eventually fell vacant.

Just now, Beckett was repairing his net, seated upon a dry rock, nicely sheltered from the wind, thoughts of the most peaceful and benevolent nature coursing gently through his brain. It was here that Charles, flagging perceptibly, at last discovered him. He half-slid down a flight of rotting steps and found himself at once in deep white sand that edged in over his shoes and tricked him by concealing sharp points of rock on which he stubbed his toes and swore. The sun was up now and the wind was tempered by the protection of the cliffs. Looking up at them, Charles saw that they were granite and immense, now pink, now purplish, now naked grey, layer upon layer of solid rock where a century might be measured in the rounding of a jagged end or the loosening of a stone. He felt dwarfed by their hugeness and age. In the shadow of cliffs such as these death appeared insignificant, even trivial, compared with the mysteries they had witnessed. He shook himself free of these thoughts, and, catching sight of Beckett's bald head bent industriously over his net, hailed it with a shout.

TEST FOUR

First Passage

The Friends of the Disabled, a charitable association devoted to the welfare of the chronic disabled and their dependants, has recently bought Torbay Hall, a seventeenth century manor house in the heart of Devonshire. Torbay Hall was once the home of John Barleycorn, the landscape artist, but following his death last year was put on the market by his grandson, who has made his home in the United States. It is a large, three-storeyed house with, in addition to the usual farm buildings, a spacious garden, an orchard, an ornamental lake and a glass-domed hothouse justly famous locally for its fine peaches.

The Friends, who have been looking for suitable premises for some time, have acquired the property with a view to converting it into holiday flats. Ordinary hotel accommodation is frequently unsuitable for guests with chronic disabilities, since it is not planned for their special needs, and it is hoped to equip

Torbay Hall with practical aids and facilities that will make it possible for even the most severely handicapped to enjoy a change of air and scene. Funds for the project have mainly been raised by private subscription, with the help of a small Government grant and a contribution towards the recreational amenities from the Atlantic Foundation, an American charity for the assistance of the physically handicapped.

It is hoped to provide short stay holidays of up to a fortnight for forty people at any one time. There will be single and double flats and two large family-sized maisonettes, also a communal dining-room and a recreation room. Further plans include the conversion of the farm buildings into a cinema and a workshop and the clearance and enlargement of the lake for use as a swimming pool.

Second Passage

It is a curious sidelight on human nature that we are usually more attracted by the bad characters in fiction than the good. Long suffering heroes and heroines meeting life's adversities with saintly forbearance do not have the same fascination for us as the outright sinner. We are able to appreciate the excellence of good characters, even to suffer with them, but they do not arouse our passions in the same way as a really evil character. It is true to say that the function of the wicked in fiction is to provide the cliffhanger situations without which we should soon lose interest. A story concerned only with thoroughly good people would be insipid, not to say boring. If we are honest with ourselves, great heroism and spectacular achievement excite our admiration not so much because the performer is good, but rather because he is good at what he does. A character who leads his men to victory against overwhelming odds, or bluffs his way out of one agonising secret service situation after another, needs the same qualities of ruthlessness and ingenuity as a successful bank robber. On the other hand, since the majority of us are content to live comparatively dull and blame-less lives, subjected to the faceless tyranny of tax officials, government legislation and big business, our fascination with the wrong-doer is a way of getting our own back. We can do little to resist the villains in our daily lives, but we can read with mounting thrills and anticipation of the triumph and ultimate downfall of fictional villains since the good, even beyond the grave, always win in the end – in stories at least.

Third Passage

It was almost noon before Ferguson reached the top of St Peter's Mount. It had been a long and arduous climb up a track made slippery by recent heavy rain, and frequently disappearing into scrub or clumps of damp bracken and patches of bog. He met no one, only a few sheep grazing alongside raised their heads inquiringly or scampered off in a flurry if he sat down to rest a moment on the grass. Once, when he looked up, a grey mist shrouded the summit and he was in two minds whether to go on or to return to the warmth and safety of the village below. "But," he thought, "it is as far down as up now, so I may as well go on." He went on, and the mist slowly drifted down to envelop him in a grey blindness, fogging his glasses and wreathing about him in chill, ghostly shapes. He waited, shivering, for it to pass, which it did almost imperceptibly to reveal at last the summit suffused with pale sunshine. From where Ferguson stood it looked no more than a grassy slope with dark patches of purple heather against the green, but he guessed that this appearance was deceptive.

He took a drink from his flask and went on climbing, his body aching with the effort, his leg muscles strained and protesting. The last few feet were the worst, smooth and dangerous, offering no secure foothold and when at length he scrambled on hands and knees to the top, he knew no sense of exhilaration, but lay panting and exhausted, a stout, middle-aged man, badly out of condition, and with little experience of hill-climbing.

After a while he stood up. The great hill stretched down to the valley, meeting a patchwork of little hedged fields, green pastures and ripening corn, looking from this distance like some giant crossword puzzle. He glanced at his watch and waited, listening. Faintly he heard the church clock in the village strike twelve.

Fourth Passage

Most London colleges have a library, with a full-time or part-time librarian, who will be able to give students information on the facilities available for consulting or borrowing books. In addition the Public Libraries give a valuable service to students attending colleges, evening classes or working on their own. Public Libraries are maintained by the City Corporation and the various London Borough Councils. They will be helpful to students who wish to further their studies by using the comprehensive library services available in the metropolitan area. These libraries have over five million books in stock, the majority of which are for loan, and there is a system of interavailability of lending-library tickets which extends throughout the metropolitan area. Reference Departments are provided for the use of those who wish to consult books and periodicals on library premises, or heavy publications such as encyclopaedias which cannot be taken out on loan.

Public library stocks are of a general nature, covering all subjects, many of them to higher degree standard or beyond. In addition, each public library in the metropolitan area specialises in a group of inter-related subjects and, through the cooperation between various libraries, their combined resources are made generally available. Moreover, through the inter-lending system of the British Library (Lending Division), it is usually possible for books not available in London public libraries to be obtained from specialist libraries. Music stocks, for example, include miniature scores and frequently records. Full details of these various services can be obtained from the Central Library in each area. Addresses and telephone numbers are listed in the London telephone directory.

TEST FIVE

First Passage

One of the greatest mysteries of the world, for which scientists have so far been unable to find any satisfactory explanation, is the Bermuda Triangle, sometimes called "The Graveyard of the Atlantic." This is an area of the Western Atlantic between Bermuda and Florida, roughly triangular in shape, where since 1945 at least a hundred ships and planes and over a thousand people have disappeared. No wreckage has been found, no bodies, lifebelts or any other evidence of disaster. It is as if these planes, ships and people had never existed. In some cases a routine radio message has been received from aircraft reporting everything in order a few minutes before all contact was lost, in others a weak S.O.S. message has been picked up and, in perfect weather, inexplicable references to fog and loss of bearings. In the extraordinary case of five U.S. navy planes disappearing on a routine mission from Florida, the rescue plane sent to locate them vanished also. There have been references to the curious white light or haze which is a feature of the sea in part of this area, and it is interesting to note that not only was this light, or streaks of light, observed by the astronauts on their way to space, but was also noted by Columbus, five centuries ago. Whether this light has any connection with the mysterious disappearances is unknown – it is just another curious circumstance as yet unexplained.

Many theories, some bordering on the fantastic, have been advanced to account for the disturbing incidents that occur in the area of the Bermuda Triangle. It has been asked whether these disappearances are caused by extra-terrestial activity, by some undiscovered source of energy, or some dimension of time or space unguessed at by Man. There is no answer and speculation continues as anxiety increases.

Second Passage

A new book by Frances Fanshawe is always an event to that vast army of readers who follow the fortunes of that well-known secret service agent, Captain Peters. Captain Peters, who first made his appearance in Miss Fanshawe's book "Death or Glory" twenty-five years ago, ought, one can't help feeling, to have earned promotion by now or, in the natural course of events, to have aged with the passage of time. But he is made of sterner stuff than ordinary mortals. He remains as daring, youthful and full of resource as ever, ready and able to find a solution to problems that would have baffled Sherlock Holmes. The new book, "Murder on the Moon", is no exception and in fact might be said to add an extra dimension to Captain Peters' already well-accredited talents. Here, disguised as an astronaut, he journeys by rocket to the Moon where a sinister plot is being hatched by an unnamed power to blow up the World. It is not explained how or where Captain Peters received his training in space travel or, for that matter, what object the enemy power have in wishing to destroy the planet Earth, since they are apparently a consortium of big business men whose interests, to say the least, must be worldly. None of this is important, however, to Captain Peters' admirers for whom "Murder on the Moon" provides the usual quota of hair-raising situations – a moon-buggy chase on the rim of a crater, the hijacking of a landing-craft, the mysterious evaporation of a space capsule – it's all here, thrills, danger, even a touch of romance in the shape of a woman astronaut, and to allay the anxiety of nervous readers, let me hasten to add that Captain Peters, as might be expected, confounds the enemy and saves the World.

Third Passage

Members attending the annual three day conference of the Eastchester Historical Association are reminded that there will be an optional half-day excursion to "Godfrey's Grave" on Tuesday afternoon, September 14th. A coach will be provided to take members as far as the Godfrey Tea-Rooms at the foot of Hunter's Hill, from where it will be necessary to walk a hundred yards up the hill to Godfrey's Grave at the top. Members who prefer to use their own transport will be welcome to join the excursion but car-owners are reminded that the Godfrey Tea-Rooms are unable to provide parking facilities for more than five cars at any one time.

"Godfrey's Grave" was designed by George Godfrey, a prosperous butcher who lived in the mid-nineteenth century. He was interested in astrology and, towards the end of his life, expended a great deal of time and energy in endeavouring to predict the exact time and place of his own death. Having reached a satisfactory deduction by means of astrological signs and symbols, he prepared for his departure to a presumably better world by closing his business and, on the appointed day, taking to his bed. When the day arrived, however, he was surprised to find himself in perfect health and so he continued for a further ten years. As a thanksgiving to the planets for having altered their courses to provide him with a longer span of life, he caused his tomb to be built on the top of Hunter's Hill. This tomb is constructed in the shape of a twelve-pointed star, with above it a domed roof representing the heavens. The points of the star are each consecrated to a different sign of the Zodiac.

"Godfrey's Grave" has been variously described by experts as "an interesting Victorian monstrosity" and "an outstanding and lovingly-executed example of man's wish to propitiate the Gods." Members of course will be able to form their own opinions and an informal discussion will be held after supper on Tuesday evening for an exchange of views.

Fourth Passage

In the hotel dining room Rosa and Andrew faced each other across a desert of white linen and gleaming cutlery. They were continuing a discussion that had begun in the train and had gone on intermittently ever since they arrived at the hotel an hour ago. The excitement of going away had prevented either of them from eating any breakfast and in consequence neither was in the best of tempers. Andrew quite frankly did not want to do any more talking till he had had his lunch. He was used to a good meal in the middle of the day and he hoped he was going to get it. He had the feeling, common among men, that any discussion is better on a full stomach. Women, he was convinced, fortified by tea and aspirins, were capable of arguing themselves into the next world. Men never discussed a matter of importance without a dinner, or at least a lunch, inside them.

Rosa, who had had her tea and aspirins in the train, could have gone without her lunch without any noticeable inconvenience. She was intent on getting her own way and was quite prepared to harry Andrew until she got it. Quite simply, she wanted to make a day trip to France, the next day if possible. There was a steamer which ran a twice-weekly service from Broadsea in the summer time. Andrew, with a kind of shame-faced desperation, was equally certain that he did not want to go. He was a poor sailor at the best of times and the prospect of a Channel crossing held no joy for him. It was unfortunate that Rosa should have seen the poster announcing the excursion just after they got out of the train at Broadsea, because he was beginning to learn that once Rosa had set her heart on a thing, it was ten to one she got it. This holiday had not been his idea in the first place, though he drew a little consolation from the fact that he had insisted on paying his own share of the expenses. To his surprise Rosa hadn't made as much fuss about this as he had expected. It was only a pity that he could not have afforded to pay her share as well as his own, and so have felt master of the situation, but it had meant getting into debt even to scrape up enough for himself.

ANSWERS TO THE TESTS

In all Tests the answers given to Paper 3 are intended as a guide, but other acceptable answers may occur to the teacher.

TEST I

PAPER 2
Section A

1. A 2. C 3. B 4. D 5. A 6. C 7. B 8. D 9. E 10. B 11. C
12. A 13. B 14. D 15. D 16. B 17. D 18. D 19. E 20. C
21. B 22. E 23. E 24. A 25. E 26. B 27. A 28. C 29. E
30. B 31. C 32. B 33. D 34. A 35. C 36. B 37. C 38. D
39. A 40. E

Section B
First Passage

41. C 42. A 43. A 44. B 45. D 46. C 47. D 48. C 49. B
50. C

Second Passage

51. D 52. B 53. A 54. D 55. B 56. C 57. D 58. B 59. C
60. C

PAPER 3
Section A

Q.1.

1. fell/slid/slipped
2. midst/pile/heap/mound
3. above/before
4. bone
5. then/so
6. still/motionless/stunned/unconscious
7. to
8. realised/calculated
9. so/two
10. wondering
11. what
12. though/although
13. chin
14. must
15. up
16. lay/sat
17. towering/rising
18. him
19. seized/taken
20. aware/conscious

Q.2.

1. Do those letters have to be/need to be answered today?
2. There is no possibility of my/me catching an earlier train.
3. What do you think the height of the tallest building in New York is?
4. The proposed merger was hardly referred to/mentioned by/the Managing Director.
5. I shall only accept that appointment if the salary is high enough/not too low.
6. Who does this briefcase belong to?
7. It's asking for trouble to increase the tax on household goods.
8. "Tell your Mother that I'll call in half an hour, Mary," said the doctor.
9. Have there been any replies to your advertisement in the local paper last week?
10. John has never been interested in music./John has never had any interest in music.

Q.3.

1. hasn't been/hasn't been feeling/hasn't been looking
2. ... the more she wants
3. ... he must have been out/away
4. might be offended/hurt/upset/angry/annoyed
5. had resigned/had given notice
6. than being interrupted
7. stopped to speak
8. had been able/allowed
9. allows him/it/or not/ gives him the money or not/gives him permission or not
10. he/tries/practises/wants to

Q.4.

1. Is it really necessary for you to catch the 9.30 train?
2. Miss Jones was awarded/given £1000 for the injuries she sustained in the car accident.
3. Being unable to speak the language, we had to make signs.
4. It can't have been John you saw at the station.
5. If he had read more, his spelling would have improved.
6. Ask Professor Smith, he's bound to know the answer.
7. Did anyone raise the question of traffic control at the Council meeting?
8. Should frozen chicken be thawed before cooking?
9. I can't think what's happened to John, he's never late as a rule.
10. In my opinion that antique mirror wasn't worth what John and Mary paid for it./In my opinion John and Mary paid more for that antique mirror than it was worth.

PAPER 4

First Passage   1. B   2. A   3. C   4. C   5. D

Second Passage   6. C   7. C   8. B   9. A   10. B

Third Passage   11. C   12. C   13. B   14. D   15. A

Fourth Passage   16. C   17. B   18. B   19. D   20. D

TEST II

PAPER 2
Section A

1. B 2. C 3. C 4. A 5. B 6. E 7. B 8. E 9. C 10. B 11. D
12. A 13. D 14. B 15. E 16. C 17. D 18. A 19. C 20. D
21. C 22. B 23. A 24. E 25. B 26. D 27. C 28. D 29. A
30. D 31. B 32. D 33. E 34. A 35. C 36. A 37. B 38. D
39. C 40. B

PAPER 2
Section B

First Passage

41. B 42. C 43. D 44. C 45. B 46. A 47. A 48. C 49. B
50. C

Second Passage

51. D 52. C 53. A 54. B 55. B 56. C 57. D 58. D 59. C
60. B

PAPER 3
Section A

Q.1.

1. were/be 2. respectable/nice/decent 3. less 4. do 5. judge
6. their 7. denied 8. expect/tolerate 9. at 10. is/seems/sounds
11. variety/collection/selection 12. must 13. forgotten/out-of-date
14. new/reluctant 15. Look 16. least 17. such 18. taste
19. fill/furnish 20. use/point

Q.2.

1. There is every likelihood/chance/possibility that my brother will get the job he is after.
2. Haven't you any other red sweaters in stock?
3. They were deep in conversation when I saw them in the corridor.
4. It is my belief he doesn't intend to do/he has no intention of doing any more business with your firm.
5. I have always been puzzled by John's attitude to his wife.
6. I shall never try to learn to ski again.
7. Where did you say the Browns lived?
8. Could Mr Jones manage Saturday, August 9th?
9. I don't think/it would be advisable to/you had better/it would be a good idea to give him your address.
10. Mr Harvey knows more about students' problems in this college than anyone.

Q.3.

1. should not have/should never have
2. will have been/will have stayed
3. would have been able/would have managed/would have arranged/would have been pleased
4. to have been found/to have been discovered

5. shall go/shall be able to go/shall want to go
6. you've asked me/you've told me/you've reminded me
7. did I know she was coming/was I to know she was coming
8. cook it yourself/you cook it
9. is it all right/would it be all right/wouldn't it be better
10. she told her

Q.4.

1. You needn't bother/Don't bother to phone me when you get to London.
2. There is no question of her going to America this year.
3. John's train is likely to be delayed because of the fog.
4. Why did you refuse to answer my question about Jane?
5. There is no room/not enough room in the garden for a swimming pool.
6. The station was near enough for us to have walked to/there.
7. We might catch the bus if we hurried.
8. He is easy to understand because he speaks so distinctly.
9. Did he give any reason why he hadn't telephoned?/for not telephoning?
10. I don't mind listening to Pop, but I like classical music best.

PAPER 4

First Passage

1. D   2. D   3. A   4. A   5. B

Second Passage

6. D   7. B   8. C   9. A   10. B

Third Passage

11. A   12. A   13. D   14. D   15. D

Fourth Passage

16. C   17. D   18. A   19. B   20. C

TEST III

PAPER 2
Section A

1. B 2. A 3. C 4. D 5. B 6. C 7. B 8. D 9. A 10. D 11. B
12. B 13. D 14. A 15. E 16. C 17. A 18. C 19. D 20. A
21. B 22. D 23. B 24. A 25. B 26. E 27. A 28. D 29. B
30. A 31. B 32. B 33. C 34. E 35. A 36. C 37. B 38. E
39. A 30. C

Section B

First Passage

41. C 42. B 43. A 44. D 45. C 46. C 47. B 48. A 49. D
50. A

Second Passage

51. C 52. A 53. B 54. D 55. C 56. A 57. C 58. D 59. A
60. B

PAPER 3
Section A

Q.1.

1. great 2. imagine/believe/think/feel 3. out 4. Let 5. mistake/error
6. as 7. hard/difficult 8. nothing 9. why 10. line/kind 11. assume/
presume 12. make 13. fault 14. before 15. matter/subject
16. for/as 17. surely/then 18. bear 19. on/upon 20. me

Q.2.

1. He gave a very bad performance in the play last night.
2. I have no idea where I left my keys.
3. At no time did we suspect that he was already married.
4. There is nothing more to be said about Peter's behaviour/the way Peter behaved.
5. That dog goes everywhere with Mr Johnson/That dog is taken everywhere by Mr Johnson.
6. Is there any possibility of his coming before Saturday?
7. There is no difference in the weight of those two sacks of potatoes.
8. Beyond sympathising, there is little we can do to help.
9. There is no admittance/admission to the Museum this afternoon.
10. He gave very accurate answers to all my questions.

Q.3.

1. been waiting/only got
2. can't hear you
3. there's anything/something the matter/there's something/anything wrong
4. must have eaten something
5. Ask him to come/tell him to come/suggest he comes.
6. we're going/we arranged to go/we're going to go
7. I'll 'phone her/I'll ring her/I'll give her a ring.
8. take it in/drop it in/leave it

9. I want/I particularly want/I'd like
10. was wounded in/was blown up in/was injured in

Q.4.

1. I shall have to cancel my appointment with Mr Higgs.
2. In Mary's place, I wouldn't have told John about the car accident.
3. The stories Michael tells about his war experiences are beyond belief.
4. There's no point in asking Mrs Simpson to sing at the concert, she's going away.
5. Haven't you any/Have you no/recollection of your life in India as a child?
6. He had heard that honey could be used as an antiseptic.
7. I spend about £200 a year on running my car.
8. His statement to the Police did not agree with the report he made to the Insurance Company.
9. Caroline owes me ten pounds for that dress she bought.
10. Nothing was further from his thoughts/mind than going to America.

PAPER 4

First Passage
1. D 2. D 3. B 4. D 5. B

Second Passage
6. C 7. D 8. C 9. C 10. B

Third Passage
11. B 12. B 13. D 14. D 15. C

Fourth Passage
16. A 17. C 18. D 19. B 20. A

TEST IV

PAPER 2

Section A

1. C 2. B 3. A 4. B 5. C 6. D 7. E 8. C 9. B 10. C 11. D
12. E 13. B 14. D 15. A 16. B 17. D 18. E 19. C 20. E
21. C 22. C 23. A 24. D 25. B 26. C 27. A 28. E 29. D
30. A 31. C 32. C 33. B 34. A 35. D 36. E 37. C 38. B
39. D 40. B

Section B

41. D 42. B 43. B 44. A 45. B 46. D 47. B 48. C 49. C
50. A 51. C 52. B 53. C 54. B 55. A 56. B 57. A 58. B
59. B 60. B

PAPER 3

Q.1.

1. far 2. possible/true 3. pay 4. confronted/faced 5. hostages/
prisoners 6. agree/accede/submit 7. demand 8. suggest/indicate/prove
9. long 10. head 11. control/command 12. no 13. responsible/liable
14. loss/safety 15. remedy/solution 16. out 17. presents/offers/has
18. problems 19. gained/acquired 20. ransom

Q.2.

1. the best she could to comfort the little boy/her best to comfort the little boy
2. interested in coming to Art classes next term?
3. didn't refuse to insure Mary's ring. I can't believe it.
4. impressed by the Prime Minister's speech.
5. any reason why Sarah is always so tired in the mornings/for Sarah always being so tired in the mornings.
6. you see him, ask him to telephone me tonight.
7. her husband tells her, Mary doesn't believe.
8. exactly an hour to fly from London to Dublin.
9. have been the man in dark glasses who murdered his wife.
10. that brief case on the table belong to?

Q.3.

1. spent/took a long time getting/reaching
2. hasn't come back/hasn't returned
3. I don't know where
4. have wanted to see/visit
5. I'll be down/ready
6. will never get/obtain. won't get/obtain
7. I've already told
8. I'd known you were coming/I'd known when you were coming/arriving/ I'd known when your plane was due
9. always saying things like that
10. why you don't start out/leave home/set out/get up

Q.4.

1. Don't you think he ever lies/tells lies?
2. What the lecturer said was inaudible to everybody.
3. This Italian phrase book came in very handy in Rome.
4. My father's disability is never spoken of/about/at home.
5. The manager has asked me to give very careful consideration to this proposal.
6. If you ask me, Income Tax will be raised in the next Budget.
7. It's impossible to find a way out of this dilemma.
8. Is Saturday the only day you can come?/Are you quite sure Saturday is the only day you can come?
9. There's no necessity to hoover the sitting-room./There isn't any necessity for you to hoover the sitting-room.
10. I'll never ask the Welfare Officer for help again.

PAPER 4

First Passage

1. D   2. D   3. C   4. A   5. B

Second Passage

6. B   7. D   8. A   9. C   10. A

Third Passage

11. D   12. C   13. C   14. C   15. B

Fourth Passage

16. B   17. D   18. C   19. A   20. A

TEST V

PAPER 2

Section A

1. C 2. D 3. A 4. D 5. B 6. B 7. E 8. B 9. A 10. C 11. A
12. D 13. C 14. B 15. E 16. D 17. B 18. D 19. A 20. C
21. B 22. D 23. A 24. E 25. A 26. D 27. A 28. C 29. C
30. A 31. E 32. B 33. B 34. E 35. D 36. A 37. D 38. A
39. B 40. B

Section B

First Passage

41. C 42. D 43. B 44. A 45. D 46. C 47. B 48. D 49. A
50. B

Second Passage

51. C 52. D 53. A 54. B 55. D 56. C 57. C 58. D 59. C
60. A

PAPER 3

Section A

1. giving 2. alarm/anxiety/consternation 3. ability 4. increasing/rising
5. steps/measures 6. remedy/improve 7. with/in 8. corresponding/
similar 9. Ages 10. literate 11. lies 12. radically/terribly/dreadfully/
drastically 13. methods/techniques 14. children's/youngster's/infant/
junior/primary/secondary 15. cope/deal 16. slow 17. attention/
encouragement 18. want/need 19. Whatever 20. ignored/overlooked

Q.2.

1. However much he suffers, he never complains.
2. Considerable anxiety is being felt/caused by the Government's decision to reduce Family Allowances.
3. The difficulties arising from the raising of the school-leaving age were unforeseen.
4. Are you in agreement with the Council's plans to widen the High Street?
5. Don't let anyone know that Sanderson has been sacked.
6. How do you feel about Capital Punishment?
7. I find it difficult to believe that Councillor Bates really means to resign.
8. I don't know much about mediaeval art.
9. There is nothing/very little evidence/to prove that Louis was in the flat on the night of the murder.
10. This Roman coin is worth/valued at/about £100.

Q.3.

1. had asked me
2. will have been
3. turn down/off
4. have kept you
5. should have seen/ought to have seen
6. have I told/have I asked/do I have to tell

7. could do
8. looked better/suited you
9. you needn't have made/baked/bought
10. shall/will see/visit/call on/telephone/ring/give a ring/call

Q.4.

1. The child's illness is the result of malnutrition.
2. I had no idea that Simon was married/The idea never crossed my mind that Simon was married.
3. I think you should shorten those curtains.
4. Derby County and Queen's Park Rangers drew one all in the match on Saturday.
5. The Masons' house must be twice as valuable/worth twice as much as when they bought it.
6. John tells me he is sitting for the Interpreters' Examination next June.
7. The local Council have decided to drop their scheme for building a shopping precinct on the new housing estate.
8. There is no point in taking all those clothes for a camping holiday.
9. The plans for the construction of the new motorway are still secret.
10. We know the kind of house we want, the only question is to find/finding the money.

PAPER 4

First Passage

1. B   2. B   3. D   4. C   5. B

Second Passage

6. C   7. B   8. D   9. B   10. D

Third Passage

11. B   12. A   13. C   14. A   15. D

Fourth Passage

16. B   17. C   18. B   19. A   20. D